Editor-in-Chief and Founder:
    Lyndon H. LaRouche, Jr.
Editorial Board: *Lyndon H. LaRouche, Jr. , Helga
    Zepp-LaRouche, Robert Ingraham, Tony
    Papert, Gerald Rose, Dennis Small, Jeffrey
    Steinberg, William Wertz*
Co-Editors: *Robert Ingraham, Tony Papert*
Technology: *Marsha Freeman*
Transcriptions: *Katherine Notley*
Ebooks: *Richard Burden*
Graphics: *Alan Yue*
Photos: *Stuart Lewis*
Circulation Manager: *Stanley Ezrol*

INTELLIGENCE DIRECTORS
Economics: *Marcia Merry Baker, Paul Gallagher*
History: *Anton Chaitkin*
Ibero-America: *Dennis Small*
Russia and Eastern Europe: *Rachel Douglas*
United States: *Debra Freeman*

INTERNATIONAL BUREAUS
Bogotá: *Miriam Redondo*
Berlin: *Rainer Apel*
Copenhagen: *Tom Gillesberg*
Lima: *Sara Madueño*
Melbourne: *Robert Barwick*
Mexico City: *Gerardo Castilleja Chávez*
New Delhi: *Ramtanu Maitra*
Paris: *Christine Bierre*
Stockholm: *Ulf Sandmark*
United Nations, N.Y.C.: *Leni Rubinstein*
Washington, D.C.: *William Jones*
Wiesbaden: *Göran Haglund*

ON THE WEB
e-mail: eirns@larouchepub.com
www.larouchepub.com
www.executiveintelligencereview.com
www.larouchepub.com/eiw
Webmaster: *John Sigerson*
Assistant Webmaster: *George Hollis*
Editor, Arabic-language edition: *Hussein Askary*

EIR (ISSN 0273-6314) *is published weekly
(50 issues), by EIR News Service, Inc.,
P.O. Box 17390, Washington, D.C. 20041-0390.
(703) 297-8434*

European Headquarters: E.I.R. GmbH, Postfach
Bahnstrasse 9a, D-65205, Wiesbaden, Germany
Tel: 49-611-73650
Homepage: http://www.eir.de
e-mail: info@eir.de
Director: Georg Neudecker

Montreal, Canada: 514-461-1557
eir@eircanada.ca

Denmark: EIR - Danmark, Sankt Knuds Vej 11,
basement left, DK-1903 Frederiksberg, Denmark.
Tel.: +45 35 43 60 40, Fax: +45 35 43 87 57. e-mail:
eirdk@hotmail.com.

Mexico City: EIR, Sor Juana Inés de la Cruz 242-2
Col. Agricultura C.P. 11360
Delegación M. Hidalgo, México D.F.
Tel. (5525) 5318-2301
eirmexico@gmail.com

Copyright: ©2018 EIR News Service. All rights
reserved. Reproduction in whole or in part without
permission strictly prohibited.

Canada Post Publication Sales Agreement
#40683579

Postmaster: Send all address changes to *EIR*, P.O.
Box 17390, Washington, D.C. 20041-0390.

Signed articles in *EIR* represent the views of the authors,
and not necessarily those of the Editorial Board.

This Generation's Rendezvous with History

EIR **Contents**

www.larouchepub.com   Volume 45, Number 31, August 3, 2018

ZEPP-LAROUCHE WEBCAST

Trump Invites Putin to Washington, Xi Jinping Tours Africa: Momentum Builds for New Paradigm

This is the edited transcript of the July 26, 2018 Schiller Institute New Paradigm webcast, an interview with the founder of the Schiller Institutes, Helga Zepp-LaRouche. She was interviewed by Harley Schlanger. A video of the webcast is available.

Harley Schlanger: Hello my name is Harley Schlanger with the Schiller Institute. I'd like to welcome you to this week's webcast, featuring our founder, Helga Zepp-LaRouche.

The big news this week is coming from Africa. China's President Xi Jinping has just toured several African countries. A very extraordinary summit—the BRICS summit and the BRICS Plus—got underway in Johannesburg, South Africa, with a very strong and important speech by Xi. A number of meetings are now underway. But it doesn't seem as though much of the leadership of the Western world is paying much attention to this at all.

So Helga why don't we start there: What's the global significance of this BRICS conference?

BRICS Summit in Johannesburg

Helga Zepp-LaRouche: The building of a new world economic order and, in that context, Chinese-African relations, are of the highest strategic importance globally. I know that many people, especially in the United States, tend to dismiss Africa, but what is happen-

Xinhua/Liu Weibing

President Xi Jinping of China (left) and President Paul Kagame of Rwanda in Beijing, China, March 17, 2017.

ing on this front is truly extraordinary. Xi Jinping's tour took him from the Emirates, to Senegal, Rwanda, and South Africa. He met with the respective heads of state of all these nations. In each country those leaders emphasized the extreme importance of the friendship between their countries—and Africa as a whole—with China.

There were many articles published in the context of this trip. Several highlighted the new practice of the "BRICS Plus," in which many developing countries that currently chair regional organizations—such as the Caribbean Community (CARICOM) and the East African Community (EAC)—are invited to participate in the summit. Many leaders of states, and other guests, were invited to participate. I highly recommend that you, our viewers, take the time and read President Xi's entire speech, which he delivered at the opening of the conference. Xi expresses directly the idea of the New Silk Road Spirit, in which he displays a kind of thinking one never hears these days from any Western leaders—certainly not from European leaders.

Xi emphasized the special role of science, calling science the inexhaustible power available for development and for improving the lives of people. He also emphasized that Africa is the region of the world that has by far the largest development potential—which is most certainly not the view most Western countries have of Africa. He evoked the spirit of Nelson Mandela, whose 100th birthday the world has just celebrated. He also emphasized that the international community is at a new crossroads, with the opportunity to build a completely new set of international relations.

The increase of trade between China and Africa, and also the increase in direct investment, is quite amazing. In 1978, Chinese trade with the entire African continent was $765 million. Last year it rose to $170 billion, and it will soon reach $400 billion per year. These trade volumes are quite significant; China has recognized that Africa has the potential to become the "new China with African characteristics." Many African leaders are extremely happy, and quite inspired, by the support from China.

It is quite interesting that there is also broad discussion in the African media and elsewhere, that whereas the West only invests in African nations having natural resources, and then only when big profits can be made, China is clearly seeking and establishing relations with countries who have almost no such natural resources but nevertheless China is investing in infrastructure including rail, roads and hydropower, and is also building manufacturing capacity with the development of industrial parks.

So this is really a big change.

India is also greatly interested in joint ventures with China in Africa. Japan wants joint investment within the Belt and Road Initiative with China in Africa. So you see, there is a potential for a completely new alignment.

This is the New Paradigm coming into being. The world is rapidly changing right before our eyes into a much better place than most people have any inkling of.

Former President Barack Obama, speaking at the University of Johannesburg's Soweto Campus, June 29, 2013.

The world can be divided into those who recognize that a new strategic model is being developed, which is rapidly being joined by many countries around the world, and those who are either indifferent, or ignorant. Or perhaps they just don't understand that the old paradigm no longer works, and that's why most of the countries in the world—the developing countries together with China and India, which represent 80% of the world population—now represent an ever-increasing part of the world economy. For the first time, the BRICS nations have bypassed the G7 in terms of GDP. What we, the Schiller Institute, are trying to do, is get the nations of the West to understand and recognize the incredible potential that lies in this new formation and rather than foolishly opposing it.

This is a very exciting development, and I encourage everyone to get on board and be part of it.

Obama Against Africa and the BRICS

Schlanger: One of the ways people can do that is to get the newly released second volume of *The New Silk Road Becomes the World Land-Bridge: A Shared Future for Humanity*, which is now available through the Schiller Institute.

Helga, you just spoke of the contrast between the old paradigm and the New Paradigm. I think that's no better illustrated than by comparing the remarks of the disgraced former President of the United States, Barack Obama, made during his visit to South Africa, with Xi's

kremlin.ru

The leaders of the five BRICS member nations at the BRICS Outreach Meeting in Johannesburg, South Africa, July 27, 2018.

remarks. President Xi said, "Every country has an equal right to development." Obama continues to say that Africa has to stick to a model of "sustainable development." A few years ago, as President, he went to Africa and told his audience that if every African had an American-style standard of living the planet would boil over! It appears as though most African governments are siding with the Chinese on this, and seeing this as an opportunity, aren't they?

Zepp-LaRouche: Oh, yes! I think that's very clear, because all the speeches by the African leaders emphasized the friendship. It's not just interest, it's a real friendship,— some, like former British Prime Minister Winston Churchill, claim that friendship does not exist among peoples. This is a sentiment that I think is absolutely foolish and wrong. You *can* start a friendship with the culture of another country, and that is exactly what we see right now.

Schlanger: Let's go to the idea of a BRICS Plus. Indonesia, Turkey, Argentina, and several other countries were at the just concluded BRICS summit. What does it look like? Is the BRICS really going to be recruiting? Are they going to bring new countries in to be part of the BRICS and join in this process?

Zepp-LaRouche: Several countries have expressed interest in joining, including Egypt. The New Silk Road Spirit is really changing the whole world. You talked about North Korea, and the Singapore summit. Now,

Libya has officially joined the Belt and Road Initiative. This is in the context of the Italian government having revived the cooperation agreement that existed during the Qaddafi government, and that is basically to compensate for the Italian colonial past with Libya. Italy is engaging in the reconstruction of Libya. There is now discussion that Libya needs to have a national army, which means disarming the militias, as a precondition for it to become a stable nation. This is a very important part of dealing with the whole African situation, because Libya has been a transport hub for many of the human traffickers who every day exploit refugees from other parts of Africa.

The Italian government is now showing great interest in working with China on many projects, some now in Libya, and earlier, on the huge Transaqua project. There is now a concrete perspective of transforming the whole world through economic cooperation on the basis of win-win relations, nations working together for the benefit of each other.

And this is also what Xi Jinping emphasized in his speech in Johannesburg, that now in the world, there is a choice between confrontation which means lose-lose, which means nobody is the winner, including in trade war; and the opposite choice of win-win, that you instead expand the size of the cake, and then everybody can have a larger piece of it.

I think this is really the crucial issue. I said at the beginning of the year that this year must be the year to overcome geopolitics. Geopolitics is not yet gone; there were many people who have just met under the auspices of the Aspen Institute, who still remain completely determined to maintain geopolitical confrontations. But I think the majority of the world is clearly moving into a new era of civilization, one of cooperation in the spirit of peace and development. I think people should just really think it through. Xi put it this way: that mankind has reached a new crossroads, and while the dangers are still there, the potentials are enormous.

A String of 'Impossible' Successful Summits

Schlanger: Several weeks ago, you pointed to the Singapore model as an example of what happens when you have that kind of cooperation, where President

Trump was working with the Japanese, the South Koreans, the Chinese, and the Russians, to get the breakthrough that led to the Singapore summit, in which President Trump met with North Korea's leader Kim Jong-un. We saw something similar with the Helsinki summit between Presidents Trump and Putin. But there's been an incredible blowback from the anti-Russian crowd, the neo-conservatives, and the geopoliticians in the United States. Trump had invited Putin to come to the United States this fall, but just yesterday it was announced that the President said the new meeting with Putin is postponed until, as Trump said, "the end of the witch hunt."

What do you make of this? This is an incredible battle. You see the effects of Wall Street, and the City of London. The whole Russiagate gang is coming down as hard as it can on Trump: Where do you think this battle stands right now?

Americans are Not Anti-Trump

Zepp-LaRouche: I think Trump has an enormous battle on his hands, and the fact that he had invited Putin to the White House for a summit meeting this fall, and now feels that the pressure is too big, I think reflects that a truly existential battle is now raging in the United States.

The U.S. Congress is behaving absolutely disgustingly. Once again there are motions to increase the sanctions against Russia, in a clear repeat of what happened last summer when Congress voted 98-2 to rein in Trump. Trump outflanked that by going ahead with the Helsinki summit with Putin.

I think this is not what the American population thinks. There was a recent survey done by *The Hill* that reports that 54% of Americans asked, were in favor of a second Trump-Putin summit, and that 61% think that having better relations with Russia is in the very fundamental interest of the United States. Now, if the people of the United States think that way, hopefully this will

President Trump is considering revoking the security clearance of former officials, including the former C.I.A. director John O. Brennan, the White House said on Monday. Al Drago/The New York Times

By Julie Hirschfeld Davis and Julian E. Barnes

find expression in the November midterm elections, and all the elected office holders who are pushing confrontation against Trump, and against Russia, will lose their seats. I think that would be a very good lesson to teach them.

Schlanger: There's another poll, which I think we mentioned last week, that shows that of the most serious concerns for Americans, less than 1% identified Russian so-called "meddling" in the election as something that concerns them.

Clearly the Congress is missing the point of what's come out on Russiagate, including even some congressmen who were doing a very good job exposing it are missing the real point here. This week, one of the things that came up, was President Trump was considering stripping the security clearance of former intelligence officials, including former CIA Director John Brennan, former Director of National Intelligence James Clapper, and others. Clapper made a statement, in a fairly direct way saying that Obama initiated Russiagate!

So this isn't going to stop, is it Helga? The exposure is going to continue. We've played a leading role in initiating it, but slowly, piece by piece, the evidence is getting out there that it was the British working with Obama intelligence officials that created and are running Russiagate.

Zepp-LaRouche: There is a new initiative by Jim Jordan and Mark Meadows, two Republican congressmen, who are demanding the impeachment of Deputy Attorney General Rod Rosenstein, saying that for nine months Congress has tried to get the Department of Justice to cooperate and turn over documents, but Rosenstein has been stonewalling for the entire period, and that this is absolutely unacceptable conduct, and that therefore he should be impeached, and a new person installed. This is very good.

There are also articles by some former intelligence

officials, like a former CIA agent who knows Brennan very well, having worked under him. He makes the argument that all former officials should be stripped of their security clearances, especially those who subsequently get themselves hired in important capacities with the media, because such behavior leads to the unacceptable leaking of secrets that these people have access to, because of their former positions. In many cases these former officials have made money that way and filled their own pockets. Therefore, they should lose their clearances.

White House Press Secretary Sarah Sanders confirmed that the security clearance stripping is being considered. I think this is very important and would be a very good thing, were it to happen.

Schlanger: On the impeachment bill against Rosenstein, Republican Jim Jordan from Ohio, one of the people who filed it, announced today that he will run for the position being vacated by Paul Ryan as Speaker of the House.

I want to move now to the economy, Helga. On one hand we see tremendous potential in the Belt and Road Initiative, and you have some figures released by China on the Chinese economy—there's an annual economic report that just came out. There's also the continued lagging and problems with the banking system in the West— more and more people warning of a collapse in the West. What do we know from this new economic report? How is it going with China and the Belt and Road?

China, Russia Lead World Away from Dollar

Zepp-LaRouche: Chinese Prime Minister Li Keqiang has just presented the annual economic report to China's State Council Executive, which announces a very robust stimulus package, focussing on the real economy. They're creating tax exemptions for investments in basic research and development; they're spending another $200 billion on infrastructure; they're advising credit institutions to make credit available, especially to small and microsize firms. This is part of the eradication of poverty. The

Chongyang Institute for Financial Studies, Renmin University of China

Sergey Glazyev, counselor to Vladimir Putin, President of Russia, speaking at the Chongyang Institute for Financial Studies in China, July 17, 2018.

Chinese government also announced a firm commitment to wipe out any kind of speculation and close down zombie firms. Li Keqiang argued that in the face of the international challenges, this is absolutely necessary.

China is preparing for the potential collapse of the Western financial system by outlawing any kind of involvement in speculation and totally focussing on the real economy, which is exactly what the West should be doing.

This is very good. It's also very interesting that Russia-China cooperation is definitely increasing. There was an important meeting at the Chongyang Institute for Financial Studies at Renmin University that included the participation of Sergei Glazyev, an economic advisor to Russia's President Putin. Glazyev emphasized the ever closer relationship growing between Russia and China, saying that if the confrontation against Russia— including new sanctions— and trade tariff measures against China continue, the only consequence will be that China, Russia, and other countries will move out of the dollar entirely, which will diminish the influence of the United States over the rest of the world.

So I think it is what Xi Jingping said. It is either cooperation or confrontation. The road to overcome the problems is cooperation, and that includes the question of punitive tariffs. As I said, the cake must be made bigger so that everybody wins. That's the way to go.

Schlanger: Punitive tariffs have the same effect as sanctions: Their effect is to force countries to creatively figure out how to do what they should do anyway, which is to develop and invest in the real economy. I think that's the point that's being made by the Chinese and Glazyev and others.

Italian Prime Minister Giuseppe Conte and President Trump at a press conference following their meeting at the White House, July 30, 2018.

Helga, I know you have an update on North Korea, continuing toward the solutions that were discussed in the Kim Jong-un meeting with President Trump. What can you tell us about that?

New Paradigm Activities and Prospects

Zepp-LaRouche: As usual, the mainstream media has tried to create the impression that nothing is working, that Kim Jong-un merely pulled the wool over Trump's eyes. That is just not true. Trump himself tweeted that he's absolutely satisfied with the speed with which the denuclearization is moving ahead. Trump also tweeted that he had a wonderful meeting with Putin, and that that was a "good thing."

Alexander Matsegora, the Russian ambassador to North Korea, has given an important interview, in which he underscores that Kim Jong-un is a very earnest and serious leader, who has made an absolutely firm commitment to go ahead with denuclearization—that everything is on a very good course.

This is very important, because there are those who would rather see World War III, than have these kinds of initiatives succeed, like Trump-Kim Jong-un, and Trump-Putin. But so far, the opposite is taking place, and this is also being confirmed by some of our friends in South Korea, who are absolutely hopeful that this process can be furthered in the near future to a very good end.

Schlanger: It also appears that the discussion process in Europe is opening up a little bit. Russia's Foreign Minister Lavrov and Chief of the General Staff, Gen. Gerasimov, had meetings in both Berlin and also in Paris with Prime Minister Emmanuel Macron. What's your take on what's happening in Europe? It seems to be rudderless, chaotic. There doesn't seem to be any firm resolve to do much of anything, but I think the discussion is beginning to loosen up a little bit. What do you think?

Zepp-LaRouche: I think there are some interesting developments in Italy. Prime Minister Conte will go and see Trump in three days; so this is obviously very important. Conte and Trump were the two leaders who demanded that Russia should be invited to rejoin the G8—which Russia may not even want to do at this point. There appears to be a very good accord between Conte and Trump, and Conte and Putin. Italy is in favor of lifting the sanctions against Russia.

This is an interesting dynamic. I already mentioned the Italian-Chinese cooperation in respect to Africa. So this is a singularly important dynamic.

There is a quite chaotic situation in France. It almost seems that somebody really wants to get rid of Macron. This scandal around his bodyguard beating people, who were already lying on the ground, is really exploding.

The situation in Germany is terrible. I think this present German government just doesn't have any idea what's going on. I can say, however, the good thing is that Chancellor Angela Merkel supported the Helsinki summit between Putin and Trump, which is one time she said something decent, so I praise her for that. It doesn't happen too often.

Interesting also is the situation in Great Britain, where Labour Party leader Jeremy Corbyn has just delivered a major speech to industrialists in which, under his party's "Build in Britain" campaign, he demanded the reindustrialization of Great Britain. He said that the City of London, which totally focuses only on the so-called financial industry, which has very little or nothing to do with industry, was clearly a mistake, as shown in the crisis of 2008.

Corbyn is demanding that major industry to be opened up again in Great Britain, in order to use more national talents, to build the things again in Great Britain that have been outsourced. When his policy was compared to Trump, he replied, "Nobody's ever said I have something in common with Donald Trump before. It's news to both of us, I suspect." Corbyn is however, clearly focussed on building up Great Britain's national economy.

So there are other interesting developments, as you say. It is chaotic. Austrian Chancellor, Sebastian Kurz will have an Africa-EU summit by the end of this year, since Austria is chairing the EU until the end of the year.

The next major event will be the China-African Union event, the Forum on China-Africa Cooperation, to be held in September in Beijing, which will be a continuation of Xi's trip to Africa, and of the BRICS summit in South Africa. At that summit will be 52 African heads of state, plus China, plus the African Union. I assume that that will mean a heightened relationship between China and Africa, which will have a major impact on this chaotic situation in Europe, given that Chancellor Kurz plans to have an Africa-EU summit.

At our June 30-July 1 conference in Germany, the Schiller Institute had a plan which I called the "Singapore Model," which is the idea that you can turn the worst kind of relationship into its opposite, if you have good will and a good plan. We said then that we should have a summit in which the Europeans would cooperate, together with China, in a crash program for the development of Africa.

These are the kinds of settings where major shifts will take place, almost every day, this year for sure. I invite you, our viewers, to not sit on the sidelines during such an historic and incredible period. If we get the United States and European nations to stop their geopolitical confrontation against Russia and China, and instead look at the potentials of cooperating in the development of Latin America, of Africa, of under-developed parts of Europe, and Asian countries, we can have a

New Paradigm of collaboration among the whole human species such as has never before existed. This is what China is actively building and putting together.

We have to put behind us the outdated, war-like Cold War mentality, the idea that the world is always a zero-sum, where one wins and one loses. We can move to a new era of civilization of win-win cooperation and a new set of international relations, in which people relate to the best traditions and best culture of other nations. We can have a dialogue on the most beautiful periods in the history of each nation, and make those known universally.

This is what I call the human species becoming adult: that our nations should stop behaving like four-year-old boys kicking each other in the shins, which is what resolving conflict through warfare is really all about. It is possible to have a completely different world, in which people relate to each other as Einstein and Planck did, or Wilhelm von Humboldt and Schiller, or other such great thinkers, respectful of and joyful in the creative potential of the other's genius.

I think that that will be the future of civilization, if we overcome this present outdated thinking of just making money for money's sake, which justifies the accumulation of riches for a fancy life for a few while tolerating misery for the many. I think we should use the potential inherent in Trump's trying to get a better relationship with Russia. Trump should revisit his initial positive relationship with China and his friendship with Xi Jinping. Everyone involved in Russiagate-Muellergate, should face their appropriate punishment because it is *they* who have committed collusion with foreign governments, not Trump.

We are all living in a very, very interesting moment in history. It's one of those periods in which the quality of individual thinking and engagement makes a huge difference. So join the Schiller Institute, work with us—we have everything to gain!

Schlanger: We're having a membership drive right now, to give people the opportunity to participate. Helga, you talk about the role of the individual. It's clear that *you've* played a role as an initiator and as a provider of great ideas that are being gobbled up all over the world, and that's what we're seeing now in Africa.

Again, I'd encourage people to go to the Schiller Institute website. Get our new report, *The New Silk Road Becomes the World Land-Bridge: A Shared Future for Humanity* and study it! Read it! Think through what it means.

After the Summit: The Future of BRICS

South African businessman Tshepo Kgadima was interviewed for EIR *by David Cherry on July 28, 2018. Kgadima is an independent political and economic analyst based in Johannesburg, South Africa. He is a former investment banker and a company director with more than 20 years' experience. He is also president and CEO of LontohCoal Limited, director of Elgacol Limited, and chairman of the Indian Ocean Rim Business Forum.*

PIB

Leaders of the five BRICS nations at the 10th BRICS Summit in Johannesburg, South Africa, July 27, 2018.

EIR: The Tenth BRICS Summit, held in Johannesburg, South Africa, ended yesterday, July 27. The BRICS association of Brazil, Russia, India, China and South Africa, is a leading institution—*the* leading institution, I think—in the formation of a new world, a world based on what I call the pastoral principle, under which each acts for the benefit of the other, as opposed to the principle of geopolitics, of each seeking to gain advantage over the other. The BRICS is a seed crystal for this anticipated outcome. Mr. Kgadima, what are some of the issues in the economic sphere that BRICS is dealing with?

Tshepo Kgadima: We have to bear in mind that when the idea of BRICS was born, to show that there can be a "new world," as you call it, in the area of geo-economics, only four nations with large economies were initially thought of—China, being the most populous in the world; India, another of the most populous; Russia; and Brazil. South Africa followed a little more than two years later, and there has been debate as to whether South Africa, in terms of its economic make-up, does fit into the BRIC nation format.

However, on the economic front, these are countries that for the next decade and more are going to continue to be *the* leading story, in terms of global economic growth, because, by and large, they still have a much younger population, and a very large population. Those are the things that you need, in terms of the working population—that it is young—but also the numbers of people where you can be able to then grow those economies sustainably over a long time to come, and effectively sustain global economic growth.

But, South Africa, in terms of how does it fit into the BRIC nations, to make a BRICS—I think a fact that has not been fully appreciated, is its positioning: that South Africa has the benefit of both the Atlantic Ocean and the Indian Ocean. That's exceedingly strategic, because a great deal of the world's trade traverses the maritime waters of South Africa, making it the most important gateway to world trade.

When you look at the BRICS nations, Brazil is a very large economy in South America, doing trade with the East, and South Africa is very key in facilitating that trade, both from the East to West, and West to the East. So it makes sense that South Africa could be included—even though it is a smaller economy—in this new league of nations, as you correctly put it, that is premised on ensuring that the principle of equality, whereby all nations can use their unique positions, their unique strengths to be able to assist the others where they are weak, and therefore not one over the other.

BRICS: Finding Each Other

The question is: Is that being achieved? I think it's going to take some years before that august goal is achieved, in that sovereign nations, by their very nature—the way they process such foreign policy initiatives—must include an ingredient of time due to domestic politics and constitutionalism. So, for these nations to really find each other to achieve their stated goal to be a new league of nations, I think we have to look at the next decade.

From the last decade, there have been some achievements, but maybe the next decade is going to be the one, really, which will prove how this group of nations will come together, and what influence they will have on particularly the western nations within the G7, as well as the role that, effectively, the G7 nations have, in terms of the Bretton Woods institutions, particularly the IMF, as well as the World Bank.

So I think it's a "wait and see." There are still some challenges ahead, though. I don't think it's going to be smooth sailing for this new league of nations called the BRICS to be able to achieve full implementation. The domestic politics in each of the BRICS countries, I think, may bring in a factor of slowing down the rate at which they might wish to move.

On the economic front, the BRICS league of nations brings in a different *flavor*, in that more than 29 percent of the world's GDP is produced by the BRICS nations. More than 40 percent of the world's population is within the BRICS. That itself is something that,

Tshepo Kgadima chairs the 23rd Meeting of the Indian Ocean Rim Association's Business Forum in Durban, South Africa, October 14, 2017.

from an economic standpoint, creates unique opportunities which these countries can leverage.

However, as much as they embrace and espouse the principle of equality and acting for the benefit of the other, I think that for some time the BRICS nations are going to need a form of husbandry, and that can only be led by the economically stronger nations. So, effectively, I see that China, India, and Russia will have to play a much more assertive role in bringing together Brazil and the smaller-economy nation of South Africa, ensuring that those goals can be achieved.

Trade among the BRICS nations has grown tremendously since its inception. But that intra-BRICS trade must not be skewed as currently is the case; we find that South Africa and Brazil have got larger trade deficits, particularly with China.

EIR: Are those trade deficits because of non-tariff barriers?

Kgadima: Yes, they are.

Increased trade with India is going to be, I think, the next big thing that will happen. But I think the question for South Africa will be: As the gateway into the rest of the continent, will South Africa—even though economically the smallest of the BRICS nations—make good use of its geostrategic position, including its position within the African continent of over a billion people? Will South Africa bring that value into the BRICS nations? South Africa—having, of course, a much more advanced economic infrastructure than any other of the countries on the continent—what role will it play?

It may take some time to get an answer to that question, because *politically* in South Africa, there doesn't seem to be any *geostrategic* thought as to what role South Africa can play within BRICS, beyond having played a role in the formation of the New Development Bank (NDB) and obtained the first branch office here in

Johannesburg. The NDB has a targeted capitalization of $200 billion; I understand that so far its capital is more than $50 billion, and it is planning to raise another $50 billion in loans.

So, when you look at that, for example, will South Africa then be able to play a much bigger role, both within the African Union (AU), within the Southern African Development Community (SADC), and to reach out, for example, to the East African Community (EAC) and the Economic Community of West African States (ECOWAS)? Will South Africa be able to play that role? Right now, I don't find that level of thought process within government, within the state, to say, "Well, this is the role that we want to play, to ensure that, indeed, we can build a new league of nations."

EIR: But what about the BRICS Plus feature of the summit, which included bringing in the heads of state that are currently chairing such organizations as the EAC, ECOWAS, SADC, AU, and others?

Kgadima: This is often nothing more than a goodwill gesture, perhaps aimed at winning friendship of the invited countries for their support in other multilateral organizations such as the UN, AU, and ASEAN.

This lack of strategic thought is delaying fruition of the goal that the leaders have set. South Africa is also a member of the Indian Ocean Rim Association—again, there is India. South Africa is a part of the Forum for China-Africa Cooperation (FOCAC). There we see that China and India have been—beyond the BRICS association—seeking to establish themselves in one form or another within the African continent. South Africa has that burden of finding out what it's going to do.

Brazil and South Africa both have a trade deficit with China, but they have a much larger trade surplus with the United States. The influence of North America, particularly the United States, also bears down on Brazil because of its location. There are a lot of pressures that still have to be thought of in more depth.

The U.S.-China Trade Frictions and BRICS

We do have to think about whether the U.S.-China trade frictions will hurt growth. Because if China slows down, we all know that it's going to have a ripple effect on the other BRICS nations. Those are some of the issues on the economic front that I think the heads of state summit should have addressed, and that they need to address.

For South Africa and Brazil, I see no reason why the two heads of state could not initiate discussions with the United States to ensure that not only do they not become part of the collateral damage, but that the trade friction between China and the United States does not affect Chinese investment in their countries, as well as in Russia. And the leaders of South Africa and Brazil perhaps need to bring the BRICS nations as a whole to engage with the United States, to ensure that trade can continue between the United States and these two other BRICS nations, regardless of who might be invested there.

The identity of the investor, whether Russian or Chinese, should not matter, because, particularly in the case of South Africa, trade between the United States and South Africa is not at the level where India, Russia, and China are doing trade with the United States.

EIR: I think you have actually made a case for the *resolution* of the trade frictions altogether, before there is a trade war. Trade wars are not only "lose-lose" engagements, they are "lose-lose-lose" in nature, taking into account, as you have, the third parties. It would be to President Trump's credit to meet with his friend, Xi Jinping, to work out "a deal," as he would say. Even trade, determined as a function of one's overall economy, need not be a zero-sum game.

Your thoughts in conclusion, Mr. Kgadima?

Kgadima: South Africa must embark on macroeconomic policy reforms that can propel its economic growth trajectory to the 4-6% levels in order to address its crisis of high unemployment-poverty-inequality. That being the case, South Africa should therefore also take decisive measures to address its gargantuan sovereign debt burden amounting to $186 billion, in order to avoid an economic and financial crisis similar to what was witnessed in Greece in recent times. This is key for meaningful BRICS membership.

tshepo@lontohcoal.com
dacherry3@yahoo.com

BRICS Countries at the Center of a New, Just World Economic Order!

by Helga Zepp-LaRouche

July 28—Inspired by the epic rise of China, a strategic reorientation of emerging and developing countries is taking place, gradually creating a worldwide economic order based on completely different principles. While the West is trying in vain to uphold the old paradigm of the neoliberal economic system, more and more nations are working with the BRICS, the Shanghai Cooperation Organization (SCO), and other regional organizations under the rubric of the Belt and Road Initiative, on the basis of win-win cooperation, and demonstrating that the world can be organized in a much more human fashion than that which we have seen from the European Union with its barbaric refugee policy.

BRICS and other heads of state at the BRICS Outreach Meeting in Johannesburg, South Africa, July 27, 2018.

"I want the Chinese model. Because what China has achieved is incredible. The way in which they have overcome poverty has never been seen in history!" These are the words of Pakistan's newly elected Prime Minister, Imran Khan, who announced at the same time that he would answer every positive step on India's part in improving their relationship, with two steps from Pakistan. This was exactly the mood at the recently completed tenth annual summit of the BRICS—i.e., Brazil, Russia, India, China and South Africa—in Johannesburg, South Africa, which was completely shaped by the spirit of the New Silk Road. It signifies nothing less than that a new era of humanity has begun, in which all nations of the world have the right to development on the basis of scientific and technological progress.

Chinese President Xi Jinping emphasized, in his July 25 speech to the BRICS Business Forum, which included Indonesia, Turkey, Argentina, Jamaica, Egypt and many African leaders—that "The international community has reached a new crossroads" and must build a whole new platform for international relations. With an inspiring cultural optimism that has been lost in Europe, Xi emphasized the crucial role of scientific progress as the engine of economic construction: "Science and technology as the primary productive forces generate an inexhaustible power that drives the advancement of human civilization." Humanity has made huge leaps from agricultural to industrial civilization, and is now facing a new round of scientific and technological revolutions and industrial transformations, and if countries seize the opportunities these offer, they could enjoy dynamic economic growth and a better life for their people.

Xi said Africa has "more developing countries than any other continent," and therefore has "more development potential than any other region in the world." The BRICS should therefore "strengthen cooperation with Africa, support its development, and make BRICS-Africa cooperation a model for South-South cooperation." This intensification will be further enhanced at the upcoming Forum on China-Africa Cooperation (FOCAC) in Beijing in September, and the integration with the Belt and Road Initiative will continue.

Indian Prime Minister Modi said that maintaining peace and developing Africa was a top priority for his government. He and South African President Ramaphosa signed an MOU for setting up a Mahatma Ghandi-Nelson Mandela Center of specialization for artisan skills and agricultural research and education.

In his speech, President Putin announced that Russia would work to energize and "light up" the African continent:

The increase in trade between China and Africa over the past 40 years has been enormous: from $765 million in 1978, trade has already reached $170 billion in 2017 and will soon be $400 billion per year. Overall, the economic importance of the BRICS states is rapidly increasing. Last year, the total gross domestic product of these countries amounted to more than $17 trillion, more than that of the EU. President Xi had paid state visits to United Arab Emirates, Senegal, Rwanda, and South Africa, and following the summit, went to Mauritius. Prime Minister Modi visited Uganda, Rwanda and South Africa. Moreover, the governments of China and India have decided to invest jointly in Africa in the context of the Belt and Road Initiative.

Another component of the new economic order is the "BRICS Plus" concept, which expands the platform for the economic association of other states and regions with the BRICS nations and for the strengthening of strategic cooperation. Among other things, it is the intention of the participating countries to increase their voting strength as an IMF bloc by increasing the number of bloc member states, thereby influencing key decisions.

Cooperation or Confrontation

President Xi emphatically took the view at the summit—with distinct reference to

CC/Chatham House

Imran Khan, Prime Minister of Pakistan.

Donald Trump's threats of tariffs on imports—that there could not be a winner in a trade war. He said that one would have to choose between cooperation and confrontation, between mutual benefit and the possibility of beggaring one's neighbor, but those who pursued this latter course would only end up harming themselves.

This effect has already been observed, since the sanctions against Russia—which many experts in that country consider to be serendipitous—have forced Russia to rebuild many areas of production that had been dismantled during the Shock Therapy of the Yeltsin years, and at the same time to deepen the relationship with China and Asia as a whole. Like the EU sanctions and those imposed by the United States Congress against Russia, Trump's threat to impose tariffs against China has the effect, apparently overlooked by its authors in their arrogance, of bringing the BRICS Plus countries together and quickening their desire for a fairer and more balanced economic system.

At a seminar given by the Chongyang Institute for Financial Studies at Renmin University in Beijing, Putin's economic adviser Sergey Glazyev pointed out that, given the poor state of Western economies—which are still focussed heavily on speculation rather than the physical economy—there is increasingly close cooperation between the Belt and Road Initiative, the BRICS, the SCO and other organizations. If the pressure on these countries continues to grow, this would only accelerate the tendency to trade using their respective currencies, as opposed to the dollar.

The Chinese government's annual report, presented by Prime Minister Li Keqiang at a recent State Council leadership meeting, shows that in terms of its do-

PIB

Prime Minister Narendra Modi of India addresses 10th BRICS Summit in Johannesburg, South Africa, July 27, 2018.

mestic economy, China is doing its best to protect the country against the effects of a new crash in the trans-Atlantic financial system. In the face of major international challenges, China will implement a package of measures to strengthen the real economy, including tax relief for investment in basic research, $200 billion in infrastructure spending, promotion of lending to small and medium-sized businesses, and decisive action against "zombie companies" or any other form of speculation.

The dynamic that is now developing around the Chinese model and the BRICS as the center of a new global economic system, is the result of decades of IMF-World Bank policies that, with their demands for so-called "structural adjustment" and "conditionalities" in developing countries, have not only prevented their development, but facilitate a gigantic transfer of capital from these states to the banks of the neo-liberal financial system. From this policy, to which, among other things, we owe a large part of the refugee crisis—along with the wars built on lies in Southwest Asia and North Africa—the BRICS and many developing countries have drawn the appropriate lessons—just as they did from the Asian crisis of 1997, in which mega-speculators such as George Soros devalued the currencies of many Asian countries by as much as 80% in mere days.

We in the West have exactly the choice that Xi Jinping has identified. We can accept the multifaceted offerings of China and, together with the BRICS and other states, help to build up Africa, Southwest Asia, and Latin America, and thereby realize a future perspective for ourselves. However, this would mean saying goodbye to the casino economy, and would require the re-introduction of a Glass-Steagall banking separation system, the creation of National Banks, and a New Bretton Woods credit system.

Or we can try to stick to the current, hopelessly bankrupt neoliberal financial system, which aims to maximize profits, at the expense of a large part of the population and developing countries. We have the choice between a new crash, this time far worse than 2008, and a financial blowout triggered by a dollar collapse if the states of the new emerging economic bloc collectively resist the U.S. confrontation.

We have a choice: Either we remember our best traditions in the United States and Europe, i.e., the American System of economics of Alexander Hamilton and the principles of the economic miracle in Germany after the Second World War, plus the tradition of our classical culture—which means working together with China and the BRICS on the development of the world—or we will have only ourselves to blame, when our cultures are very soon exhibited in the museums of Africa and Asia, as examples of societies that were morally unfit to survive.

zepp-larouche@eir.de

DIRCO ZA

President Xi Jinping of China addresses 10th BRICS Summit in Johannesburg, South Africa, July 26, 2018.

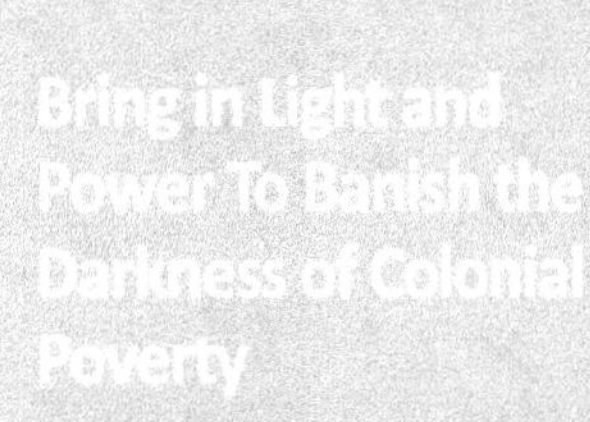

Stop Club of Rome Genocide in Africa!

by Lyndon H. LaRouche, Jr.

with a new preface by Helga Zepp-LaRouche

is now available in flowing text ebook and paperback editions from Amazon.com and Google Play Books.

Today, the ideas presented in this book are rapidly being adopted and implemented around the world by more and more governments and institutions. Most importantly, the concepts in this book actually work! Poverty *can* be eliminated from the list of problems facing mankind.

This and dozens of other important EIR books are now available from Amazon.com and Google Play Books.

Leibniz and the Stradivari Violin— Or, the Contrapuntal Dance of Beauty and Truth

by David Shavin

The June 22, 2018 issue of EIR *covered the 1696 contest over Leibniz's second transcendental curve, the brachistochrone, and Isaac Newton's bizarre response, in the article, The Case of Sir Isaac Newton—or, What Was God Thinking? This present story, insofar as it deals with the birth of the transcendental curves, may be considered a "prequel."*

July 26—When Gottfried Leibniz was confronted with developing a strategy for Peter the Great's Russia, his mind went for, what to him was, the obvious: European culture and Chinese culture were peculiar bookends of the whole Eastern hemisphere. So, of course, Russia could have no better, or more lawful, strategic mission than to maximize the world's development by conjoining these separate cultures into something qualitatively superior to Europe, China or Russia, separately. Leibniz's mind insisted upon going to the highest level necessary to find where a beautiful idea cohered with a truthful idea.

Today, beyond the bankrupt and dirty geopolitical thinking of the recent decades, there exists the imminent, objective possibility of exterminating world poverty, turning deserts into gardens, and earth-forming the moon. No matter how often this technological capacity can be shown, an underlying and unnatural cynicism, born of decades of submission to ugliness, persists in Western culture-with words and looks to the effect of "But, you know, it is never going to happen." The emo-

*Gottfried Wilhelm Leibniz
(1646-1716)*

tionally blunted response may acknowledge some abstract moral duty to wipe out poverty, but the excitement and joyful anticipation of such a mission is strangely absent. However, it is a beautiful mission. We may actually have to get happy about the work ahead.

We, today, are challenged, then, to be inspired by beauty so as to fight to locate and realize the underlying truth of what is possible, and now, quite necessary. It is to that end that we examine a curious few weeks that Leibniz spent in Florence, Italy, and the amazingly beautiful and truthful fruits of those few weeks. This is the never-before told story of Leibniz's role in the birth of both the beautiful, lased, "bel canto" Stradivarius violin, and the powerful scientific family of transcendental curves.

Leibniz in Florence

Leibniz, age 43, visited Florence, Italy, in November and December, 1689. He had sufficient time to appreciate, and be inspired by, the Santa Maria del Fiore Cathedral and its famous dome (cupola).[1] Leibniz gave classes, on his new developments in physics and his methods of analysis, to the two sons of the Medici Duke, Cosimo III, and to their tutor, Baron Rudolf Christian von Bodenhausen. The classes went quite well, and Leibniz entrusted to Bodenhausen's care his manuscript copy of *Dynamica et potentia*, to be prepared for publication by Bodenhausen. Within seven months of Leibniz's viewing of that cupola, for which the catenary curve plays a major role, Leibniz announced that he had solved the historic catenary puzzle.

At the same time, Cosimo and his older son, Prince Ferdinando, had commissioned a set of instruments—two violins, two violas and a cello—from Antonio Stradivari, age 45. Ten months after the visit, Stradivari delivered to Prince Ferdinando his revolutionary violins, a breakthrough that is now designated as the first of the "Long Strads." After almost a quarter of a century of violin-making, in 1690 Stradivari altered his design to create a full, round, free and yet structured sound, one that amazed hearers.[2] Looking back, violins prior to 1690, those of the Amati family, of Maggini, of Stainer, would be remembered for their sweet sound or possibly their big sound, but it appeared paradoxical for powerful and sweet sound to co-exist in the same instrument. It was Stradivari who solved the puzzle of maximizing both freedom and structure, in a violin described by Joseph Joachim as having, uniquely, "a more unlimited capacity for expressing the most varied accents of feeling."[3] Stradivari had made a violin in the image of

Detail from Raphael's "The Ecstasy of St. Caecilia" 1516, Bologna. While the rudimentary violin still has flat surfaces, the key is the large and well-formed C-bouts pinching in the middle, attempting to fashion a clearly defined "head" and "chest" register. This was completely absent from centuries of predecessor stringed instruments, such as the rebec.

mankind. He would fully concur that he was, indeed, echoing the Creator.

The Violin Project Before 1690

After centuries of string instruments such as rebecs et al., a qualitative breakthrough occurs around 1500. There appear stringed instruments with well-defined c-bouts that sufficiently separate an upper chamber and a lower chamber—the violin. Tedious official histories of the violin will find safe ground in citing a contract for Andreas Amati to provide violins in the 1550s for a royal wedding; or even pushing the origin story earlier, by citing a painting from the late 1520s with something

---

1. See "The Secrets of the Florentine Dome" by Karel Vereycken, 2013: http://schillerinstitute.org/educ/pedagogy/2013/vereycken-dome-1.html *and* "Brunelleschi's Dome: The Apollo Project of the Golden Renaissance" By N. Hamerman/C. Rossi, *21st Century Science & Technology*, July-August 1989: https://21sci-tech.com/Articles_2014/Brunelleschi.pdf

2. *Antonio Stradivari: His Life and Work*, by W.H. Hill: "The year 1690 is perhaps one of the most interesting epochs in Stradivari's career; it certainly marks the most complete innovation as regards form, construction and proportions of the violin which took place in his work … We refer to the creation of the 'long Strad'."

3. Joachim was Johannes Brahms' favorite violinist. His quote in context is: "While the violins of Maggini are remarkable for volume of tone, and those of Amati for liquidity, none of the celebrated makers exhibited the union of sweetness and power in so pre-eminent a degree

as Giuseppe Guarneri and Antonio Stradivari. If I am to express my own feeling I must pronounce for the latter as my chosen favourite. It is true that in brilliancy and clearness, and even in liquidity, Guarneri, in his best instruments, is not surpassed; but what appears to me peculiar to the tone of Stradivari is a more unlimited capacity for expressing the most varied accents of feeling. It seems to well forth like a spring… as if Stradivari had breathed a soul into them, in a manner achieved by no other master."*The Salabue Stradivari*, W.E. Hill, 1891, pp. 7-8.

looking like a violin. But the story is told with the underlying conceit that the violin must have started somewhere, but wherever it did start, it was rather accidental—sort of like an ape-man deciding one day to stand up straight. It is remarkable that Raphael's drawing of a violin in 1516 is simply ignored.

Once attention is drawn to Raphael's Florence of around 1500, it becomes rather unmistakable that the development of the violin was by design. Particular attention should be paid to the three years that Raphael and Leonardo da Vinci were both in Florence, 1504-06. Leonardo was no stranger to the design of instruments. The idea must have been based upon an attempt to unpack the workings of the amazingly full, powerful and beautiful sound of what we will designate as "bel canto" singing.[4] Beautiful evidence of such exists in Luca della Robbia's 1430s sculpture for the Cathedral of Florence, in which he captured the mouth positions

Luca della Robbia's Cantoria, sculpted for the organ loft of the Cathedral of Florence.

of singers fully engaging their head register with their chest register. A character such as Leonardo would surely have been challenged to investigate the unique dynamics of such a laser-like event, even if it were happening inside a human being. It takes little to imagine a consequent interest in fashioning organic models, such as wooden models, of such dynamic couplings of two-chamber systems.

The first step in investigating this claim, however, is not to feverishly search for some "smoking pistol" proof, but rather to experiment by singing with the engagement of both head and chest registers; and then to fashion a mapping of your own discrete alterations that bring a qualitatively-new resonant coupling into play—one that neither chest nor head could produce individually. That there is a higher-order, dynamic interplay in multiply-connected—in this case, doubly-connected—spaces should, then, not be doubted. Admittedly, what one can succeed in unpacking about such a development may yet be a bit more challenging.

From no later than 1516 and continuing until 1690, there were fine developments in violin-making, centered around four generations of the Amati family of

---

4. See *A Manual on the Rudiments of Tuning and Registration,* Schiller Institute, 1992, on "bel canto" singing, with discussion on the "aperto, ma coperto" (open, yet covered) sound; the "voca impostata" (well-placed voice); and the properties of a round, full shape, while still clear—due to the lasing focus of the mask.

Least Action: The Soap Film

The soap film displays the least-action surface, a catenoid, connecting the two circles that serve as boundaries. As a first approximation, imagine a wire-frame boundary of two spaces, a "head" and a "chest" region, conjoined. Very modest alterations of the boundary conditions can result in dramatic changes in the soap film's delineation of least-action. (If you wish to begin training your mind to think about three-dimensional "least-action" surfaces, examine some of these soap bubbles: https://www.youtube.com/watch?v=YdneSMKObls from 08:50 to 11:00; and then go get some soap film, design some wire frames, and "go to town"!)

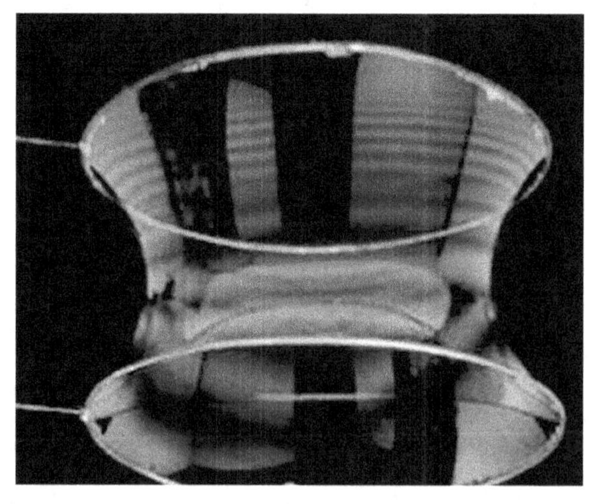

Cremona, Italy. Antonio Stradivari learned his craft from Nicolas Amati's workshop in the 1660s Cremona, either directly as a student, or indirectly from craftsmen trained and influenced by Amati. A good luthier (violin-maker) would literally hear the potentialities in the spruce and the maple by rapping the plate of wood, and making a mental map of the wooden plate's aural topography. One could form a map of the tonal qualities of the plate, not unlike the way a sculptor has to perform some sort of evaluation of the topography of the piece of marble he is to work with. Stradivari evidently developed a strong capacity for what might be called aural imagery.

However, the two wooden plates to be matched up for the front and back of the instrument were only the boundary conditions of the system.[5] Somehow, Stradivari, for his 1690 breakthrough, must have developed a sense for the unseen and unheard aerodynamics of the coupling of the head and chest registers.

Leibniz's Year Prior to Florence

Leibniz's scientific developments in the year prior to his 1689 visit to Florence provide our best insight into his discussions in Florence with Bodenhausen's group. In 1688, Leibniz was challenged to unpack and further develop the working of Johannes Kepler's solar system. While on a three-year trip (1687-1690), away from his home in Hanover, and to Austria and Italy, he examined a review of Newton's 1687 *Principia* in the Leipzig *Acta*. Leibniz recognized that the mathematical bowdlerization of Kepler's rich physical-science method of investigation was harmful, and he took up the challenge. He published his "Essay on the Causes of the Celestial Motions" in the *Acta Eruditorum*. In early 1689, he expanded that essay, using his differential and integral calculus to de-mystify, e.g., the causal workings of gravity. Leibniz viewed Newton's "action at a distance" formulation of gravity as having a medieval, occult quality—designed so as to inhibit scientific investigation.

Leibniz then had extensive dealings in Rome with members of the scientific institutions, where he found the axiomatic assumptions of René Descartes were also stultifying progress.[6] His "Phoranomus" dialogue, composed in July 1689, reflects his intervention there. He characterized Descartes' physics as dealing with dead matter, or "vis mortuam," and counterposed to it actual "vis viva," or living matter, for physical investigations.[7] Treating the physical world as inert stuff may make for a tidy package, but, as with Newton's mathematicization project, Descartes' approach was yet another version of reductionism. Rather, it was the scientific investigator's mind that had to rise up to the complexity of the subject of investigation and had to form whatever more advanced conceptual tools were necessary to account for the richness of nature.

For Leibniz, any motion worthy of investigation was one accomplishing work, and was one changing the world in which the motion itself was occurring. Leibniz's very title, "Phoranomus," itself is a term referring to the laws of what might be called substantial motion—as opposed to perhaps the more prevalent term, "kinematics," which would imply any sort of undifferentiated motion. The Greek word "phora" means to bear, as in to carry. Hence, space is not evacuated and void of directionality. Rather, some pathways through space work more efficiently than others. Leibniz would further develop this in his work on the catenary.

It is in this period that Leibniz expresses the need, as Bernhard Riemann would later put it, to investigate the hypotheses that lie at the basis of Euclid's geometry. It is not only a matter of removing false assumptions, but, even more, of figuring out why correct ones are correct. Beyond Euclid, Leibniz thought that the even more fruitful work of Greek physics and geometry, as reflected in the work of Archimedes, had to be put on a higher basis. In Leibniz's "Phoranomus" dialogue, his character Baldigiani describes the project:

> Hence you will conjoin a science most useful to life with great personal benefit, if you bring us such bright light in the great darkness we are in, and impose laws not only on statics, which Archimedes had formerly put under bondage, but

---

5. Simply within the level of the plate, a curious use of the "golden section" seems to set Stradivari apart from the Amati tradition. See "Stradivari's Golden Mean," http://wlym.com/archive/fusion/tcs/19890102-TCS.pdf, pp. 62-63.

6. Also in Rome, Leibniz met with Filippo Grimaldi, establishing an ongoing collaboration with him on cultural exchanges with China. (Later, after developing more of his transcendental curves, he would suggest to Grimaldi's missionary team that they should educate the Chinese emperor and his court on his "geometria situs" methods.)

7. When Leibniz got to Florence, he communicated with Francesco Redi, Cosimo III's head physician. Leibniz's conceptual drive for "vis viva" put him in Redi's camp vs. Buonanni. (Redi showed that Buonanni's "spontaneous generation" theory was wrong; that life could only be generated from other life.)

also on universal phoronomy and the explanation of moving forces.

Charinus, another character in "Phoranomus," explained:

> In geometry and numbers, I observe evident principles of unavoidable necessity. Everything gets explained by parts of the same magnitude variously transposed. But the moving forces seem to me to possess something incorporeal I do not know of … Therefore, every time I would conceive the powers of machines, I was confronted with something unexplored and not admitting of any image.

Hence, in his next work, *Dynamica*, Leibniz states:

> I judged that it was worth the trouble to muster the force of my reasonings through demonstrations of the greatest evidence, so that … I might lay the foundations for the true elements of the new science of power and action, which one might call 'dynamics'.

Leibniz actually coined the word *dynamica* to address the power that was at play, though not visible. There were operative principles at work which were not visible, but were determinable—metaphysical, but not occult.

Leibniz in the Court of Florence

Florence's Duke Cosimo III de Medici employed Baron Bodenhausen to tutor his two sons, Grand Prince Ferdinando, then twenty-five, and his brother, Prince Gian Gastone, eighteen. Ferdinando was already quite passionate about music and was a patron of the arts. The year before, in 1688, Ferdinando had brought to Florence, Bartolomeo da Cristofori—the future inventor of the pianoforte. Cristofori was given a significant salary, with the assignment of restoring the ancient instruments in the collection of the Medici and of developing

Painting by Antonio Domenico Gabbiani. 1685.
Prince Ferdinando de'Medici at the keyboard with his musicians.

Painting by Joseph Lecurieux.
Nicolo Amati (1596-1684)

Bartolomeo Cristofori (1655-1731)

new instruments. (Cristofori was also to play in Ferdinando's chamber music group, the "Virtuosi da Camera.") Of some note, Cristofori had, evidently, lived with and trained under Nicolo Amati in Cremona, probably in the late 1670s—at the same time as, and in the same neighborhood where Stradivari made violins in his studio.[8] Certainly, Ferdinando had an expressed interest in developing new instruments; and it were

____

8. The 1680 census in Cremona listed one "Christofaro Bartolomei" in the household of Nicolo Amati. Feathers get ruffled because he is listed as thirteen years old, whereas Cristofori was twenty-five. However, it would have been illegal for him to live there at that older age, so such an altered entry is not hard to understand.

likely that the man he especially sought out to hire, Cristofori, also was trained by Stradivari's teacher.

Perhaps more astonishing is that at the same time as the hiring of Cristofori, in 1688, Ferdinando moved Luca della Robbia's Cantoria sculptures of the "bel canto" singers crafted in 1438, into the Museum of the Florentine Cathedral.[9] On their 250th anniversary, the sculptures were taken down from the modest choir stalls in the church and, after a fashion, given new life. The issue of a lased, "bel canto" physical phenomenon was clear and present for Bodenhausen and Ferdinando, one year prior to Leibniz's visit and two years prior to Stradivari's breakthrough.

Leibniz arrived in Cosimo III's court some time in November, 1689. Then, no later than November 27, he paid a visit to Vincenzo Viviani, the pretended leading scientist of the court of Florence and a dyed-in-the-wool follower of Galileo. (As a youth, during Galileo's last three years, Viviani was his assistant. Later, he would be the first editor of Galileo's works.) Leibniz was cordial with Viviani. Afterwards, Leibniz reported that Viviani was "highly surprised" at his scientific methods, as Viviani "did not expect analysis to go so far" as Leibniz had developed it. Leibniz added: "It is true that it is only recently that it goes that far."

Aside from Bodenhausen, Leibniz's key collaborator in Florence was Antonio Magliabecchi, the head of Cosimo's library. While Magliabecchi didn't penetrate Leibniz's scientific work as deeply as Bodenhausen, he was a passionate man of letters, who had a remarkable relationship with the wealth of Renaissance culture. (He had a collection of 50,000 books and manuscripts. It was said that he had studied most or all of them, and that he could recite innumerable passages and quote the page of the book.) He had no trouble recognizing the breadth and power of Leibniz's mind, and he would play an ongoing role in radiating Leibniz's works throughout Italy.

Antonio Magliabecchi (1633-1714)

It was Bodenhausen who delved into Leibniz's method of scientific investigation. After several weeks together, Leibniz, rather remarkably, assigned Bodenhausen the task of editing for publication his manuscript, *Dynamica et potentia*, leaving the manuscript with Bodenhausen. Clearly, Leibniz was rather impressed with the level of comprehension and mastery displayed by Bodenhausen.

As part of his classes and discussions on *Dynamica* for Bodenhausen, and Ferdinando and Gian Gaston, Leibniz worked through some of his inventions for the two royal students. When one situates the intense four-to-six-week period of lectures and discussions, amongst the other two known factors—the fresh attention paid to the Cantoria sculptures and the unmistakable presence and influence of the remarkable architectural wonder, the cupola—the potential for all sorts of progress is apparent. As part of this, the type of "analysis situs" approach to the most efficient and powerful pathway—that is, the unique "least-action" pathway—for a coupled bi-chamber region, is quite credible and even rather likely.

The Fruits of Leibniz's Visit

After Leibniz left Florence on December 22, 1689, Bodenhausen's group pursued Leibniz's *Dynamica* on their own. Bodenhausen reported to Leibniz on the ongoing scientific discussions.[10] It was during this period, the spring and summer of 1690, that Stradivari crafted his new "bel canto" instruments that were delivered to Ferdinando in early September, 1690. For his part, Leibniz solved the scientific puzzle of the catenary no later than July, 1690, seven months after his visit to the cupola.

First, however, Leibniz had to complete his assigned genealogical research for the House of Hanover, amongst the d'Este family's records in Modena, Italy.

---

9. The sculptures had spent 250 years adorning a small choir stall in the Cathedral. Now, they were given a prominent place in the Museo dell' Opera del Duomo, next to the Cathedral.

10. From 12/31/1689 to 8/12/1690, a period covering Stradivari's work, there are twenty exchanges between Bodenhausen and Leibniz. (The two exchange a total of seventy-six letters before Bodenhausen's death in 1697.) Also, during the eight months in question, there are seventeen more letters between Leibniz and Magliabecchi.

Leibniz arrived there on December 28, 1689 and spent five weeks there. Of some interest, his host, the Duke of Modena, Francesco II d'Este, played upon a Stradivarius cello, which Stradivari had personally delivered to the Duke in Modena less than four years earlier.[11] This might have been the first occasion that Leibniz heard an instrument by Stradivari, though there is no record of his interchanges with the Duke.

One distinct possibility for Stradivari hearing of Leibniz's insights would have been through Francesco II. By this scenario, Leibniz would have heard, in Francesco's cello, a wonderful instrument, but yet one not quite up to its potential. Francesco personally knew Stradivari and could have easily communicated to him. The only "stretch" here would be—barring an actual direct meeting of Leibniz and Stradivari—whether Francesco would have understood Leibniz's thinking well enough to communicate something truly insightful for Stradivari. The direct link between Florence's Bodenhausen/Ferdinando team and Stradivari still remains the more likely avenue.

Leibniz, having completed his research for his Hanover rulers on their potential link with the d'Este family, left Modena on February 2, 1690. His trip home to Hanover, Germany included stops in Venice, Italy and Vienna, Austria. He arrived home in the latter part of June. His report that he had solved the catenary puzzle appeared in the July, 1690 *Acta*.

Meanwhile, back in Cremona, Stradivari worked on his new instruments. Stradivari had actually received the commission for the Medici instruments in 1684;[12] however, while he completed other commissions within months, he appears to have only crafted his first three new "long Strads" six years later, in the spring and

Antonio Stradivari (1644-1737)

summer of 1690. Once he made his breakthrough, he worked rapidly. In October, 1690, he worked on the two violas, completing the set of five instruments.[13] It is not known why Stradivari delayed work on the Medici commission, but given Ferdinando's expressed interest and commitment to new instruments, Stradivari might well have been experimenting for five years without achieving a satisfactory breakthrough. Regardless, it suggests that, after more than five years of delay, Stradivari's bold new conception was realized in the first few months of 1690. There is no record of what discussions and/or deliberations occurred between the Bodenhausen/Ferdinando group in Florence and Stradivari in Cremona during that time.

On September 19, 1690, Stradivari received a letter from the Marquis Ariberti of Cremona, who, in 1684, had ordered the instruments for Cosimo III, reporting: that he had delivered the two violins and one cello to Prince Ferdinand; that the court was quite struck by the sound of them; and that the alto and tenor violas were eagerly awaited. "All the virtuosi gathered in his court are of the same sentiment that they are perfect … In earnest, I must beg you to commence at once with two violas, that is to say the tenor and contralto, which are lacking, to make complete the entire concerto"—that

<hr>

11. Francesco's sister, Mary Beatrice, had just been deposed, a year earlier, as Queen of England, in what was titled "The Glorious Revolution." She was the wife of James II. (The set of instruments ordered from Stradivari, for James II in 1682, have never been located.)

12. In 1775, Paolo Stradivari sold his father's tools and relics to Count Cozio di Salabue. Later, Cozio's grand-nephew, the Marquis Dalla Valle, came to possess a 1684 letter by Stradivari as to the order for the instruments for the Grand Duke of Florence, Cosimo III, the order placed by the Marquis Ariberti.

13. The moulds and paper templates still exist for the instruments. Stradivari's handwriting, inscribed on the walnut mould, records the "forma nuovo" used for the "Gran Principe di Firenze"—dated October 4, 1690 for the Contralto Viola and October 20, 1690 for the Tenore Viola. He had been urged to finish these last two on September 19, 1690.

is, to complete the entire concert of five instruments.

Bernoulli's Catenary Contest

In the May, 1690 issue of *Acta*, Jacob Bernoulli posed the challenge of figuring out the catenary, or "hanging rope," curve—that is, to derive and define the curve assumed by a rope, or a chain, that is suspended at both ends. The catenary distributes the effort, of supporting the links of the chain, equally throughout the curve. As the most stress-free pathway, it was found to be invaluable in Brunelleschi's solution to the puzzle of erecting a dome to span such an unprecedentedly large opening.[14]

While Bernoulli was well aware of Leibniz's works and methods, it is not clear whether Bernoulli's choice of a catenary contest had any link to awareness on his part that Leibniz had just visited the cupola in Florence. Their correspondence seems to begin in earnest only after Bernoulli's May, 1690 challenge on the catenary. Prior to that, Bernoulli's relationship with Leibniz was confined to his close following for several years of Leibniz's works in the *Acta*. Otherwise, in the period before the May, 1690 challenge, Jacob Bernoulli's dialogue partner on the catenary was his younger brother, Johann, whom he introduced to Leibniz's methods.

Bernoulli had immersed himself in Leibniz's analytical methods, beginning with the historic, 1684 "New Methods." In the May, 1690 *Acta*, Bernoulli was actually responding to a challenge posed by Leibniz in September, 1687, called the isochrone, or equal time, curve: "To find the curve of descent along which a heavy body descends uniformly and approaches the horizontal by equal amounts in equal time intervals."[15]

Jacob Bernoulli (1645-1705)

Huyghens had immediately sent in an answer, which was published in the next issue of the *Acta* along with a more extensive treatment of isochrone by Leibniz. It was Bernoulli's study of that material that prompted his May, 1690 article, at the end of which, Bernoulli posed his catenary challenge. Bernoulli had worked through Leibniz's new methods, including his calculus, and had followed Leibniz's attempts to educate Huyghens on Leibniz's more powerful generalized methods, which had been based upon Huyghens' prior work, and now he wanted to join the dialogue as an active participant. Bernoulli's fortunate and particular choice of the "hanging-rope" problem may have been the one truly timely coincidence of Leibniz's 1688-90 period.

For many years, both Leibniz and Huyghens had been well aware of the catenary problem. In Huyghens' case, some forty years earlier, he had proved that Galileo's solution—that the falling-rope curve was the parabola—was not, and could not, be correct. Neither Huyghens nor Leibniz had gone any further in solving the problem until 1690. Immediately after arriving home in June, 1690, Leibniz composed and submitted his article on the catenary, published in the July, 1690 *Acta*:

> This problem, proposed by Galileo and famous since his time, has not yet yielded to solution … I have attacked [it], which I had hitherto not attempted; and with my [analysis situs] key, happily opened its secret approaches. However, this problem is a little more involved than my former one [on the isochrone] and displays a certain singular use of our method; thus I have thought it worthwhile, before publishing my solution, to give time also to others for exercising their skill. By this, as by the Lydian stone,[16] we shall know

---

14. For a treatment of the catenary and its link to the cupola, see Bruce Director's "The Long Life of the Catenary: From Brunelleschi to LaRouche," *Fidelio,* Spring 2003.

15. Contrary to some commentators' confusion, this is not the same as Huyghens "tautochrone," or same-time, curve. Leibniz was posing, what were the boundary conditions (here, the beginning and end points), or what was the shape, of a curve whose constraint is that, while the body falls under its own weight, it falls equal amounts in height, in equal

amounts of time. (Obviously, the lateral distances traversed, and the areas subtended, do increase.)

16. In ancient Lydia, a pure silver or pure gold coin would leave a standard mark on a special black stone. The "touchstone" test of suspected coins would leave different marks if they weren't up to standard.

the best methods; which bears much on the improvement of the science.

His first letter to Jacob Bernoulli (Sept. 24, 1690) modestly assured him: "I think I can satisfy you regarding the catenary curve as well." Leibniz's powerful discovery would introduce scientists to the amazing corollary, that all the powers and properties of logarithms were derived from, and subsumed under, the catenary—that the catenary was a sort of physical algorithm, that underlay the human-engineered, cultural device called a logarithm.[17] The contest ran for one year before the June, 1691 *Acta* published Leibniz's historic work, along with the submissions of Huyghens and the two Bernoulli's.[18]

After the birth of the "bel canto" Stradivari violin and of the catenary curve, Leibniz made a forecast regarding the higher-level methods that he had introduced, leading to the development of the transcendental curves, e.g., the catenary, the logarithmic spiral, the cycloid and the tractrix. On December 27, 1691, he wrote to Johann Bernoulli's student and patron, Guillaume de l'Hôpital, about what was variously called "analysis situs," "geometria situs" and "characteristic situs"— that "unless made believable through examples of some importance, it would be regarded as just a vision. Nonetheless, I see in advance that it will not fail." Leibniz had his reasons for such confidence.

The Beautiful Dome vs Euclid's Ass

Earlier, in October, 1690, Leibniz had written Bodenhausen of his success with the catenary, and

Domenico Tempesti
Vincenzo Viviani (1622-1703)

Bodenhausen informed Leibniz (Jan. 19, 1691) that their collaborator, Magliabecchi, would communicate Leibniz's results to two stubborn defenders of Galileo, who had resisted Leibniz's scientific advances:

Mr. Magliab promised me to advise Gulielmini in Bologna and Marchetti in Pisa, who will not be able, alongside the loud-mouthed of this town [Viviani, of Florence], to smash this chain [the catenary!]—especially the second one, who shouts everywhere that analysis and algebra are only fatigue-work for the ultramontanes [meaning, for the Germans, Leibniz and Bodenhausen] who lack genius …

Bodenhausen personally provided Viviani with Leibniz's catenary solution; however, Viviani simply refused to look at it. His hero, Galileo, had been proven wrong, and Viviani was apparently too sensitive to learn any better. Rather, he chose to lunge flight-forward at Leibniz.

Viviani had been embarrassed at the court of his patron, Cosimo II, both by Leibniz's work with Bodenhausen and the princes, and, again, by Leibniz's catenary solution. He represented to Cosimo that he could turn the tables on Leibniz. On April 4, 1692, Viviani sent to Leibniz a "curious" problem he had devised. In sending it, Viviani used a code name (an anagram of "postremo Galilei discipulo," or Galileo's last disciple) and Cosimo instructed his ambassador in Vienna to forward the "Geometrical Enigma" to Leibniz in Hanover. It was much ado about very little.

Leibniz solved it the day that he received it, and included a letter that explained how his analytical methods and calculus made such problems easy to solve. However, Leibniz was being polite. Viviani had actually constructed a problem that involved finding the surface area of a hemisphere with four rectangular windows cut out, as if it were the top of some building. Compared with the fascinating problems of the shape and construction of the Cupola of the Cathedral, Viviani's foray into this contest with Leibniz was pathetic.

---

17. See Pierre Beaudry's translation of Leibniz's "Two Papers on the Catenary Curve and Logarithmic Curve": https://www.schillerinstitute. org/fid_97-01/011_catenary.html and Bill Ferguson's translation of Johann Bernoulli's work on the catenary curve: http://21sci-tech.com/ Articles%202005/Bernoulli.pdf. Also, an account of Ferguson's class on the catenary: "Experimental Metaphysics: Leibniz's Infinitesimal Captive," by Michael Kirsch and Aaron Yule. https://science.la-rouchepac.com/publications/dynamis/issues/october06.pdf

18. Given Newton's bizarre submission to the later, 1696 Brachistochrone Contest, one can be thankful that he didn't simply suspend a rope, trace out the curve on a piece of paper, and send it in. In 1690/1, Newton, rather prudently, kept silent.

He could not have picked an example that would put him in any worse light. Leibniz explained to Ferdinando that Viviani's non-proof was a "simple mode of exhibiting a figure obtained by the intersection of a sphere and a cylinder." This matter of Archimedean statics had already been conquered and superseded in Leibniz's discussions in Florence with Ferdinand—but Viviani was clueless.

Magliabecchi wrote to Leibniz about Viviani's intrigues in court over his challenge to Leibniz:

> They have concealed the problem, not only from Sig. Baron B[odenhausen] and me, but from all our friends … Surely he had it sent to you, illustrious Sir, because he thought that you … were unable to solve it, and he could then fill the court with the scandal that you are ignorant; and the Sig. Baron and me, ignorant and malignant, for celebrating you so much. That is why he used all means in order to hide it.

Further, Bodenhausen related Magliabecchi's description of Viviani's faction: "They always do all their things through cabal, and with a villainous politics; nobody could possibly be more malignant than this geometer [Viviani]: an ass who does not know anything besides Euclid."

There is a deep irony in the way that Viviani attempted to strike out against Leibniz. Leibniz became the first man in history to master the catenary curve, the curve at the heart of the secret of the construction of the Cupola in Florence, and a breakthrough in the new science of transcendental curves. Viviani, the leading professor of Florence, imagined that a hemisphere with round windows cut out—that is, with cylinders cutting orthogonally through the hemisphere—could somehow give Leibniz pause for thought. Nothing of the beautiful, inspiring challenge of the crowning of the Cathedral in Viviani's own backyard seems to have ever touched his heart or creased his brow.

Stretto: LaRouche's Echo of Leibniz

Lyndon LaRouche had a comparable experience to that of Leibniz's 1689 visit, in his own encounter with the Cathedral in visiting Florence in 1988. It became a central metaphor for LaRouche in delineating the relationship between truth and beauty:

> This connection is illustrated with exemplary appropriateness by a case I have often referenced since 1988, the lesson to be adduced from Brunelleschi's successful construction of the famous cupola of the Santa Maria del Fiore Cathedral of Florence. I continue to emphasize that example, not merely because I succeeded, during 1987-88, in rediscovering a principle which Brunelleschi had used, with his foreknowledge of its success, in effecting a process of construction which had been thought physically impossible. The principle he used to secure that success, was the same catenary principle which Leibniz, more than two centuries later, was first to identify as the expression of the universal principle of physical least action. Here, art and science were the same principle.[19]

LaRouche continued, that in Brunelleschi's solution of the doming of the Cathedral,

> … truth as a method of art, and truth as uniquely a method of physical principle for successful construction, coincide. To succeed in sculpting a figure caught in mid-motion, the mind of the sculptor must feel the impact of what Leibniz defined as a universal physical principle of least action, just as Brunelleschi settled upon the use of the catenary, in the form of a hanging chain, a form of matter in motion even when it appears stilled, to enable the process of constructing the double wall of the cupola. The point was not that the finished cupola reflected the catenary form, but that the ability to construct those walls depended upon the principle of action expressed during each and every momentary phase of the ongoing process of construction of the still yet to be completed cupola.

With this, we come to our quadruply-connected conclusion. First, LaRouche's argument for "the mind of the sculptor" feeling "the impact of what Leibniz defined as a universal physical principle of least action" might equally well be made for, second, the mind of Stradivari in divining the least-action pathways of the conjoined upper and lower chambers of the violin.

---

19. "Believing Is Not Necessarily Knowing" by Lyndon LaRouche in 1/17/2013 EIR. http://www.larouchepub.com/lar/2003/3002believe _ know.html

Third, the mind of Leibniz, the master of "analysis situs," might discern the role of the catenary in mentally recreating the construction of the Dome.[20]

____

20. This author had the opportunity to pose to LaRouche the role of Leibniz's visit to Florence as an inspiration for his subsequent solution of the catenary. As I recall, he was a bit surprised that Leibniz had actually been there. I imagine that the thought triggered memories of the fruitful effect that the cupola had upon him. Then he quickly and happily concluded, "Why, of course!"

And, finally, LaRouche's argument for a Leibnizian "vis viva" approach to sculpture and architecture was crafted, independent of any knowledge on his part of Leibniz's actual experience with the cupola three centuries earlier. So, the fourth level, the mind of LaRouche, a master of the "analysis situs" as to how ideas causally transform the physical world, could identify the role of Leibniz himself participating in that process, in mentally reconstructing the relationship of truth and beauty.

The 1690 'Tuscan' Stradivari Violin

Stradivari's "long Strad" model introduced the "bel canto" violin and was his key design over the next decade. But he continued perfecting his violin for three more decades. There are many recordings with his "bel canto" violins, but very few with the first one.

Gioconda De Vito performed on the 1690 "Tuscan" Stradivari violin, on loan from the Italian government beginning in 1953. Here she performs the famous Bach "Chaconne" in 1957. While there are limitations to the recording—and, further, the full, surrounding sound of a Strad must be experienced live—still, some comparison can be made with her 1952 performance on a fine 1762 Gagliano violin. Same player, different instrument: https://www.youtube.com/watch?v=ZBQBF3c_T6w. In this 1952 performance, De Vito is soloist in the Brahms Violin Concerto, conducted by her close collaborator, Wilhelm Furtwängler. (Again, there are significant recording limitations, but one can still enjoy the poetic collaboration.)

Of some note, in 1953, De Vito actually performed a Brahms sonata on the "Tuscan" Strad, with Furtwängler himself accompanying her at the piano. They played for Pope Pius XII, at Castel Gandolfo, the Summer retreat of the Pope. Pius had specifically requested the particular Brahms sonata. Furtwängler was impressed with the Pope's knowledge of the classical composers, and learned that playing the violin had played a key role in the Pope's life.

The 1690 Tuscan Stradivarius Violin.

Finally, the Pope wanted to hear De Vito perform Mendelssohn's Violin Concerto, which she did on the Strad in 1957—but Furtwängler was no longer alive. Earlier, in Italy in 1952, Furtwängler had conducted the Mendelssohn with De Vito as soloist, playing her Gagliano. (Indeed, it is likely that the Pope had heard of this performance, had heard this particular recording, and, as a consequence, had requested the Mendelssohn.)

Rome's Accademia of Santa Cecilia produced this video on the "Tuscan" Strad. Fabio Biondi performs part of Biber's "Passacaglia" on it. Acoustics are a bit echo-y, but there is no mistaking the unique sound of this violin—the simultaneous combination of beauty, strength and expressiveness.

View at: https://www.youtube.com/watch?v=ddGgqiYLo&index=2&list=OLAK5uy_lKWwblKV_rucQGsJtxWz790MIK6kqR0_o&t=0s

With this level of contrapuntal developments, it is time to turn to John Keats, who addressed the matter in his "Ode on a Grecian Urn":

Heard melodies are sweet, but those unheard
Are sweeter; therefore, ye soft pipes, play on,
Not to the sensual ear, but, more endear'd,
Pipe to the spirit ditties of no tone …

Epilogue: the Real 'Glorious Revolution' of 1688/9

Gottfried Leibniz actually did owe a modest debt to Isaac Newton, though it had nothing to do with calculus. Newton's project to turn Johannes Kepler's work on the solar system upside-down, to formalize it in mathematical equations, was actually part and parcel of the takeover of England and its transmogrification into an Empire—called by the victors, the "Glorious Revolution" of 1688/9. But Newton's project also usefully impelled Leibniz in 1688 to come to Kepler's defense and to develop physical science with his new and powerful "analysis situs" methods.

Leibniz's method was based upon a lawful relationship between the Creator and what was created, the creations. While Euclid and Newton had their underlying axioms, Leibniz's method assuredly contained an underlying hypothesis, stemming from Plato, who announced in his *Timaeus* dialogue that God is good. That means, amongst other things, that the Creator has a lawful relationship with mankind. In a lawfully created world, one made by a good Creator, there is neither any part, nor any way to figure out a part, except as part of a whole. Any investigation has to account for fundamentals, from the top down. Humans can and should conform their actions, so as to be in the image of the way the Creator acted—the universe, galaxies, solar systems, life and humans were created.

For Plato, Kepler and Leibniz, this proper investigation of the world is the way we truly discover who we are; and it brings us closer to our Maker. For all three, there is a fundamental coherence between the harmony of the solar system and the harmonic tuning of humanity's ear. This coherence may be somewhat of a miracle; but it is also practically the definition of "beautiful." The fountainhead of beauty is a world where a good God created mankind in his image. As such, Keats concluded his above-cited "Ode": "Beauty is truth, truth beauty—that is all / Ye know on earth, and all ye need to know." Hu-

EIRNS/Kathy Wolfe

Norbert Brainin (left) and Gary Strum examine 1709 Freffuhle *Stradivarius from Cremona.*

manity really does have an inner compass in the difficult pursuit of truth, and that is its passion for beauty.

Leibniz's passionate search for truth, in his 1688-9 development of Kepler's physics, happily intersected his trip to Florence and its beautiful domed Cathedral. It is hard to deny that two glorious breakthroughs were, indeed, the fruit of those weeks in Florence—the lawful development of the family of transcendental curves, and the revolutionary "bel canto" Stradivari violin, with its union of power and beauty. Here we have the conjoined case where:

(a) the beauty of the Dome impels a truthful scientific breakthrough, and
(b) the truth-seeking of Leibniz's new physics spreads the growth of beauty.

This does qualify as the actual "Glorious Revolution" of 1688-9—and one that may serve as a model for humanity today, not only in performing our duty to develop Africa, the globe and the solar system, but to restore to our beleaguered culture an honest and open relationship with beauty.

You're Human!
Do You Know What That Means?

by Robert Ingraham

PART SIX
We conclude this report with a discussion of Mankind's present and future prospects.

VI.—Spirit of the Belt and Road

> *Getting along with Russia is a good thing, not a bad thing … The world wants to see us get along.*
> —President Donald Trump,
> March 21, 2018

As we have explored in the preceding sections of this report, to be human means to act on the future. This is the singular distinguishing feature which sets the human species apart from all other creatures. Effective action, interventions which create new possibilities for human advancement, all arise from within the individual human mind (human soul). The self-generating spark, the power of hypothesis—a power capable of overturning past axioms and opening up new insights into the lawful ordering of the universe—is the essence of human nature. Of all the creatures which inhabit the Earth, only Man has this capability. That is who we are. Through such human interventions, we change our future course, transform our present environment, and redefine the meaning of mankind's past accomplishments. Our discoveries of principle act on the past, present and future simultaneously, outside of clock time, so to speak.

Shall we have a future? Shall we accept the mission to *ensure* that a productive future exists for yet unborn generations of human beings? This is a decision that each individual must resolve for himself or herself. What shall I make of my life?

Space

On August 25, 2012, the space craft Voyager 1 left our solar system, having passed through the region of plasma known as the *heliosphere*, beyond Pluto. Voyager 1, still operational and still transmitting data back to Earth, is now 13.2 billion miles from the sun, as it heads toward the constellation *Camelopardalis*. Thus, mankind has already extended our reach out into the galaxy.

Since the flight of Yuri Gagarin in 1961, 561 human beings have traveled beyond the Earth's atmosphere into outer space. More than forty different nations have sent their citizens into orbit, including Brazil, South Africa, Kazakhstan, Malaysia, Vietnam, Mongolia, Mexico, Afghanistan, Syria, and Iran. As of June 2018, 70 different nations have established space agencies, including Indonesia, Egypt, Nigeria and Pakistan. Of these nations, nine currently possess an orbital launch capability. These are Russia, the United States, France, Japan, China, India, Israel, Iran and North Korea.

Three nations—America, China and Russia—have launched men and women into orbit.

Twelve human beings have walked on the moon.

There are six humans in space right now (3 Americans, 2 Russians, 1 German).

At the same time, humanity has also reached out much further into the solar system. During the last

NASA

Soviet cosmonaut Yuri Gagarin (foreground) and his back-up pilot Gherman Titov aboard a bus taking them to the Baikonur Cosmodrome. Gagarin became the first human to orbit Earth in outer space, aboard Vostok 1, launched April 12, 1961.

forty years, we have successfully landed spacecraft on Mars, Venus, asteroids and comets, as well as on Saturn's moon Titan. We have orbited Mercury, Saturn, Jupiter, and visited Uranus, Neptune and Pluto. In addition to the mission of Voyager 1, Voyager 2 is also exploring the outer reaches of our solar system and will soon pass into the interstellar medium. And the New Horizons mission, which left earth in 2006, has just passed Pluto and will begin exploring the Kuiper Belt in 2019.

Through the deployment of a vast array of "deep-space telescopes," the universe itself has begun to reveal some of its revolutionary secrets, in the process posing paradoxes which overturn much of what is currently accepted axiomatic mathematical belief. All of these discoveries will require new Keplers, new Einsteins, new Leonardos to unravel the hidden principles of universal creation.

These are not "machines" traveling to these outer regions of our solar system or investigating distant stars. This is the Mind of Man reaching out into the galaxy. All of the rovers, orbiters, telescopes and other pieces of technology were invented by human beings, and this often involved solving very difficult conceptual problems. The discoveries which are being made all now become a part of human culture—subjects of human deliberation and future action. This is the power of human thought, extending its sovereignty out beyond the biosphere of the Earth. This is the first step in mankind's extra-terrestrial future.

This is our common destiny. It is a project which encompasses all of humanity; it is not the monopoly of any

In NASA's last manned landing on the Moon, Apollo 17 Astronaut Eugene Cernan salutes the American flag, December 1972.

one nation. This is our shared mission which binds every nation and every human being on Earth together.

Present and Future Challenges

In past chapters of this report, we have discussed several of the galactic threats and extinction crises which have confronted mankind in the past. Those dangers are with us still. In one sense, modern human civilization has existed, so far, in a "grace period." During the last 20,000 years we have never experienced a VEI8 super-volcano; we have never experienced an asteroid impact with global consequences (let alone the effect of the one which struck Mexico 60-plus million years ago); we have never experienced either a galactic or solar event which seriously threatened the atmosphere or biosphere of our planet.

Since the (temporary) retreat of the glaciers roughly 11,000 years ago, we have existed—more or less—in a relatively stable terrestrial environment. It is as if the universe is giving us a break to get our act together, to make preparations to meet the challenges that lie ahead. Yet, change, dramatic change, is a feature of our universe, and we must prepare for the future.

One recent example should suffice to illustrate the necessity for human scientific advancement. In 1994 the comet Shoemaker–Levy 9 struck Jupiter. Before its impact it broke up into fragments, the largest of which, fragment G, was estimated to have released an energy equivalent to 6,000,000 megatons of TNT (600 times the earth's nuclear arsenal) upon impact, creating a crater almost exactly the diameter of the Earth. If, instead of Jupiter, Shoemaker–Levy 9 had hit

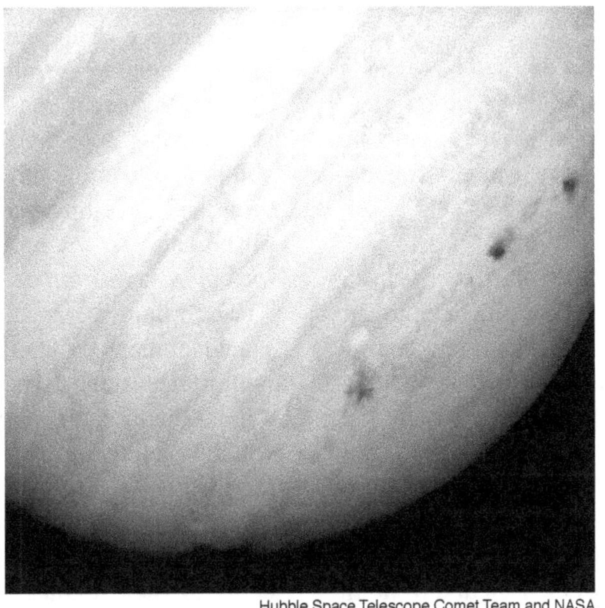

Brown spots mark impact sites of comet Shoemaker-Levy 9's fragments on Jupiter's southern hemisphere.

the Earth, mass extinctions and a collapse of human civilization would have been a certainty.

That said, it must also be forcefully asserted that under no circumstances is it fated in-the-stars for the human species to go extinct. Unlike the system of oligarchical monetary empire, mankind has no inescapable Appointment in Samarra. Yes, current and future threats to our existence are very real, and if we sit here—bonobo-like—wallowing in gluttony, avarice and lust, the fate of our species is sealed. Any human culture which is governed by entropic principles—a self-imposed entropy which is contrary to the self-organizing creative nature of the universe—will not survive.

Saint Augustine, in his writings against the Manicheans, demonstrated that evil is not an inherent part of God's creation, nor of actual human nature. Scientifically, the correct synonym for evil is *entropy*, as we see in all self-destructive oligarchical systems. Such entropic systems cannot survive in our self-developing universe. But the human species can.

America, Russia and China

At the recently concluded Helsinki summit, President Trump stated:

> We (the United States and Russia) will have discussions on everything from trade to military to missiles to nuclear to China, we'll be talking a little bit about China (and) our mutual friend President Xi Jinping.

As we pass midsummer 2018, the recent discussions among Presidents Donald Trump, Xi Jinping and Vladimir Putin have unleashed what can only be accurately defined as a global Peace Initiative. The meetings and discussions among these three leaders have been unprecedented. The three most powerful nations in the world are joining together in the name of world peace. Nothing like this has happened before in human history.

China's leadership is fully committed to the economic development paradigm of the Belt and Road Initiative. Vladimir Putin has made great strides in rebuilding the wreckage of Russia's economy. Donald

Trump is acting to overturn the pro-war policy axioms which have dominated the United States since 9-11. All three leaders are acting with great courage, and they are working together.

For the foreseeable future, this dynamic will continue; its effects will deepen and broaden. Were increasing numbers of citizens to actively and publicly proclaim their support for this new paradigm of peace and economic development, this will spell the end of British geopolitics. It will deliver a fatal blow to the imperial system of usury, exploitation and war.

From Syria to Ethiopia to Bolivia, hope is arising, and a great turning point in human history stands before us. This is a moment in which willful human intervention is critical, where the actions of individual human beings shall determine which path is taken. This is where the concept "acting on the future" becomes concrete: Shall each of us find new powers within ourselves to intervene now to aid in bringing the New Paradigm into existence? This is an individual personal responsibility.

kremlin.ru

President Trump (left) and President Putin at press conference following their historic summit in Helsinki, Finland, July 16, 2018.

Immortality

In one sense, it is legitimate to state that the physical existence of the human species is *potentially immortal*, and there is truth in such an assertion. Unlike all other earthly creatures, the human species possesses an anti-entropic cognitive nature. Only mankind has the ability to overcome threats of extinction, to continue to grow and develop as a species to ever-loftier accomplishments. *Yet, there is a far more important way to look at this question of immortality.*

Each human mind, as an embodiment of the individual human personality, already possesses a potential immortal existence. The still-living power of the human mind—the human soul—embodies a species-nature which reaches out over centuries, long after the flesh has died.

Lyndon LaRouche has spoken of this eternal quality of the human mind, of the reality that the creative discoveries of a human individual—that is, the mental action of discovery itself—never dies. He has called this the *Simultaneity of Eternity*, but I ask the reader to not just give this phenomenon a label and file that label away, but to consider the implications of that staggering feature of our species and to ponder what this implies as to our proper role in the universe.

Perhaps a personal note will make this clearer. There have been several books that I have read in my lifetime that have profoundly shaken me with such a *noëtic* power. One was my first reading of Dante's *Commedia*, another was Blaise Pascal's *Provincial Letters*, and a third was the *Leibniz-Clarke Correspondence*. There have been others. These were not words-on-a-page. They were not merely "lessons" to be learned. In each case, the living mind of the author was grabbing me, shaking me, as if he were in the room, sitting in front of me. And, he was—an intangible human mind engaging another human mind over the span of centuries—debating, taunting, helping, and always challenging—an *agapic* dialogue that exists but can not be touched, or smelled or audibly heard. It is a compositional dialogue, as new thoughts and new discoveries emerge.

It goes further. Take John Keats' *On First Looking into Chapman's Homer*. Not only is he presenting an inner dialogue, within his mind, with both Chapman and Homer, but he is bringing you, the reader, into this timeless simultaneous multi-dimensional conversation. The mind of the author is still affecting the future, centuries after his physical death. *The idea, the act of discovery, still exists as a living power within the universe.* It is immortal, everywhere and at all time.

An even more powerful example is great musical composition where the inner process of discovery is even more explicit, more intimate, and the dialogue of the most profound essence. An attentive immersion in Beethoven's Opus 132 seizes both the mind and the heart, in ways which are disturbing, uplifting, devastating, and even painful. This is where the real essence of human beauty, human immortality, might be touched.

Perhaps, you have had such experiences. Your predicates might be different from my own, but every human being has intimate moments of truthful reflection and insight where they catch sight of the beautiful potential

Voyager 1 image of Saturn from 5.3 million km, showing Saturn's shadow on the rings.

which binds us all together. It is this intangible "touching" of the eternal which is the basis for all optimism. This is the realm from which all human creativity arises. It is daunting,—even terrifying—and many turn back, out of fear. But it is just at such moments that creative breakthroughs are made—timeless moments wherein one's own sense of identity might "change in an instant" and where it is possible to discover and deploy new powers from within one's self.

This is the lesson of Prometheus, tortured and chained to a rock, his flesh decaying—yet eternally powerful in what he has unleashed—and continues to unleash—within the universe.

The Wondrous Future

Ten thousand years ago, human beings lived in the final stages of the Paleolithic era; 5,000 years ago, we were creating machines from bronze. Socrates lived 2,500 years ago. Columbus discovered America 526 years ago. And a mere 49 years ago human beings walked on the moon. It is stunning. It is breathtaking. It requires, in the words of Friedrich Schiller, nothing less than an "Ode to Joy."

Yet! —to take this even further, consider that the true revelation is not merely the brief span of time within which this has all been accomplished. There is a more crucial quality, one of "acceleration," that has characterized it. The apostles of Jesus used to speak of the "quickening of the soul." Contemplate for a moment the evolutionary anti-entropic "quickening" of the human species.

With his discovery of the principle of *Potential Relative Population Density*, Lyndon LaRouche has defined a measurement to judge the worth or worthlessness of any given human culture, much as Yahweh judged Sodom. LaRouche's concept is not a formula, nor a mathematical measurement. It defines a process, a dynamic, and the rate of change in that process defines the ability of any given society to survive and perpetuate. As LaRouche correctly insists, for the human race to continue to exist as a potentially immortal species, there must be an ongoing anti-entropic increase in the upward rate of potential relative population density—i.e., a continual non-linear acceleration of mankind's cognitive intervention into the universe.

This has implications for science, music, and economics—and most importantly for the requirement to encourage the emergence of individual human genius.

Our only pathway to progress into the future is to accelerate the *noëtic* power of Mind within the heavenly biosphere. That is clearly what the universe desires from us. And there is nothing, nothing, other than the murderous monetary policies of empire and a suicidal culture permeated by the Oligarchic Principle, to stop us. Our species role is not defensive, i.e., to prevent extinction. There are great tasks—and challenges to be met—as we move forward, to create a beautiful future for all human beings.

The universe is now beckoning us. It really is. If you listen closely you can hear it … not with your ears but with your mind and your heart. Human creativity and *agapē* are of one piece. They define who we are and the nature of the universe we all inhabit. The human race shall reach new galaxies we can, as yet, barely see. We shall create new forms of matter we haven't even yet imagined.

Our first step is to eliminate the last vestiges of oligarchism which still infect human society, and then begin to move out into the stars. As Pip advised Estella, it is time to abandon the culture of death, throw open the curtains, and go out into the sunlight.

Thus … the Spirit of the Belt and Road.

Partial Bibliography for the Series

Bogucki, Peter & Crabtree, Pam J. *Ancient Europe 8000 B.C.–A.D. 1000.* Charles Scribners Sons, New York, NY, 2004.

Cevik, Ozlem. *The Emergence of Different Social Systems in Early Bronze Age Anatolia.* Anatolian Studies, Vol. 57, Archaeology of Ancient Anatolia, 2007.

Childe, V. Gordon. *The Bronze Age.* Cambridge University Press, 1930.

Cohn, Samuel K., Jr. "The Black Death: End of a Paradigm," *American Historical Review*, Vol. 107, No. 3 (June 2002).

Deniston, Benjamin, "Mass Extinctions as Shadows of Anti-Entropic Growth: Macro-Ecological Revolutions" (2012), available at https://www.larouchepub.com/eiw/public/2012/eirv39n12-20120323/15-20_3912.pdf and "What's the Matter with the Economy?: Have You Asked Your Galaxy?" (2012), unpublished.

Finlayson, Clive. *The Humans Who Went Extinct.* Oxford University Press, 2009.

Gordon, C.D. "Procopius and Justinian's Financial Policies," *Phoenix*, Vol. 13, No. 1 (Spring 1959).

Hartwell, Robert. "A Revolution in the Chinese Iron and Coal Industries During the Northern Sung, 960-1126 A.D.," *Journal of Asian Studies*, Vol. 21, No. 2 (February 1962).

Joffe, Alexander H., "The Rise of Secondary States in the Iron Age Levant," *Journal of the Economic and Social History of the Orient*, Vol. 45, No. 4 (2002).

Laiou, Angeliki E. *The Economic History of Byzantium.* Dumbarton Oaks Research Library and Collection, Washington, D.C. (2002).

LaRouche, Lyndon H., Jr. "A Report on an Unusual Production," LaRouche PAC, January 14, 2014. Available at https://www.larouchepub.com/eiw/public/2014/eirv41n04-20140124/13-18_4104.pdf

LaRouche, Lyndon H., Jr. "COUNT-DOWN," LaRouche PAC, February 5, 2014. Available at https://www.larouchepub.com/lar/2014/4107countdown.html

Lewis, John S. *Rain of Iron and Ice: The Very Real Threat of Comet and Asteroid Bombardment.* Addison-Wesley, Reading, MA (1996).

Lucas, Henry S. "The Great European Famine of 1315, 1316, and 1317," *Speculum,* Vol. 5, No. 4 (October 1930).

Morley, Neville. *The Roman Empire: Roots of Imperialism.* Pluto Press, London, New York (2010).

Russell, Josiah C. "Effects of Pestilence and Plague, 1315-1385," *Comparative Studies in Society and History*, Vol. 8, No. 4.

Theodossiou, E.; Manimanis, V. N.; Mantarakis, P.; Dimitrijevic, M. S. "Astronomy and Constellations in the Homeric Iliad and Odyssey," *Journal of Astronomical History and Heritage,* Vol. 14, No. 1 (March 2011).

Usher, Abbott Payson. *The Early History of Deposit Banking in Mediterranean Europe.* Harvard University Press, Cambridge, MA (1943).

Usher, Abbott Payson. *A History of Mechanical Inventions.* McGraw Hill, New York (1929).

Vernadsky, Vladimir I., "Human Autotrophy," *21st Century Science & Technology* (Fall–Winter 2013).

Weeks, Lloyd R. *Early Metallurgy of the Persian Gulf: Technology, Trade, and the Bronze Age World.* Brill Academic Publishers, Inc., Boston, Leiden, (2003).

Note: The first part of this series may be found here, and subsequent parts are in the following, consecutive issues of Executive Intelligence Review: *Part II; Part III; Part IV; Part V.*

April 22, 2001

LAROUCHE IN 2004: A DRAFT POLICY

Launch a Sudden Recovery

by Lyndon H. LaRouche, Jr.

Early this past week, I warned against yet another lunatic act of Nietzschean desperation by U.S. Federal Reserve Chairman Alan Greenspan. This time, I presented, in summary, my own three-point policy for halting the world's presently accelerating economic collapse, and for launching a durable process of general economic recovery.

Those proposals were:

1. Increase the general interest-rates, rather than lowering them.
2. Apply the principles of "Chapter 11" bankruptcy organization, to ensure the continuity of functioning of those public and private institutions which make an essential contribution to the general welfare.
3. Launch a "Franklin Roosevelt" style of economic recovery measures, through regulated flow of newly created credit to relevant public and private enterprises.

I emphasized the relevance of such precedents as both the FDR recovery policies, and those comparable 1931 proposals presented to the Friedrich List Society of Germany by Dr. Lautenbach, which latter, if they had been adopted openly by the German government, could have prevented Adolf Hitler's coming to power.

My own proposal early last week, won approval from some knowledgeable persons, from several nations, who are notable for their superior past performance in both financial and economic analysis and

forecasting; however, they warned that the lunatics presently in charge of international financial policy, were likely to continue with foolish policies, such as Greenspan's, which would accelerate the presently ongoing, global financial catastrophe. I regard those reactions to my proposal, as a fair description of the implications of an increasingly deranged, and desperate state of mind of most leading U.S. and other policy-makers today.

Nonetheless, it was and remains my view, that by putting forth that proposal at that moment, I might contribute to creating the circumstances in which my proposal could win adoption among a significant number of leading and other nations. It is ideas which have been placed on the table at a time when their adoption seemed most unlikely, which are, usually, the indispensable first step toward securing their sometimes early adoption. I explain the deep principle involved in making such preemptive policy-proposals, and, after that, add some vital information on the actual implementation of an economic-recovery proposal such as my own.

The Principle of the Flank

In virtually all childish games, the play is regulated by a rigged, pre-fixed set of rules. If adults were childish enough to play the game of life by such fixed rules, society would either collapse, as it often does, or the people would break those rules and adopt more appropriate, new ones. Thus, it is often rightly said, that "a done deal" is a "mafia"-style game, which, on past performance, usually puts some of the players early into the cemetery. All games played by fixed rules, either collapse more or less immediately, or simply slide into their lawful ruin by a corrosive process of attrition.

In politics, as in military science, the alternative to doom, is a sudden change in the pre-set rules, which often brings victory to the side which has the good sense to see a reality which exists outside the world as it is seen according to the generally accepted notions of existing rules. The easily recognizable name for such successes in breaking the assumed rules of the game, is called "flanking" the problem. The famous von Schlieffen documented the way in which Frederick the Great of Prussia flanked and whomped, twice in the same day, a superior, highly professional Austrian army, which latter thus suffered the misfortune of playing by a set of pre-fixed "blackboard" rules of the game, at Leuthen.

In the practice of science, the discovery of a universal physical principle, is exactly such a "flanking" action against the stubborn fool who is still playing at the blackboard according to pre-set rules of mathematical physics.

It is also a fundamental general principle of all successful scientific practice, that all great scientific discoveries of principle, occur as a result of the eruption of a crisis in a generally accepted, present way of thinking in terms of some fixed set of rules. My associates and I have repeatedly cited an historically interlinked pair of Classical examples, that of the way in which Kepler discovered a principle of universal gravitation, and that of the way in which Fermat created a revolution in geometry by discovering a principle of quickest time, rather than shortest distance.

Any such crisis in the juxtaposition of fact and belief, takes a form which may be described mathematically, as a fatal error in the equivalent of currently generally accepted mathematical physics at the blackboard. What one's mathematics at the blackboard says should happen, not only does not happen, but any attempt to describe the contradictory reality by existing mathematical rules leads to a disaster of the type called a fundamental paradox, within the existing practice of science.

The same principle applies, with full force, to generally accepted forms of that mathematics-at-the-blackboard used to describe and defend what is taught as economics in virtually every university classroom and boardroom in the U.S. today. The reason I have been consistently successful, over more than three decades,

EIRNS:Stuart Lewis

Lyndon H. LaRouche, Jr. "Call it Lyndon's rule in strategy: When no longer in doubt, flank!"

in my long-range economic forecasts, whereas all of my opponents in that field have consistently, and now catastrophically failed, is that, as the saying goes, "they were not playing with a full deck." They were playing according to sets of rules, which, while generally accepted among most influential circles, did not correspond to the real world.

Sooner or later, as has now happened, the fact that my critics "were not playing with a full deck," has caught up with them. If they are intelligent and sane, they will admit their mistake; if they refuse to admit their mistake, they have no choice but to go utterly mad, as hopeless Federal Reserve Chairman Alan Greenspan has done.

Whether the response is, in one case, a sane one, or, in another, not, nearly everything each has believed about economics, up to now, especially "free trade," "globalization," and "new economy," has been proven, in reality, to have been dangerously absurd.

Now, therefore, how do I react to all those well-meaning people, who advise me to win others to my point of view "without alienating them by insulting their intelligence," without pointing out to them the silliness of rules of economics and politics in which they continue to believe? How do I react to those who insist that I should address people "on their own level," and "in terms they are willing to accept"? What a damned fool I would be, if I did not reject such seemingly friendly advice! If Frederick the Great had accepted such advice, he would have been whomped at Leuthen, instead of the Austrians he defeated.

The key to my outstanding successes as an economist, and as a strategic forecaster, has been, that I do not "play by the rules," and have not damaged my mind, as so many have done, by thinking "according to the rules." For anyone who wishes to know, that explains why I have acted, as I did, early this past week, in presenting an absolutely necessary economic-recovery policy, which even those who agree with the policy, think could not be implemented within the foreseeably near future.

Call it Lyndon's rule in strategy: When no longer in doubt, flank!

The able, but errant Clausewitz, who was not up to the standard of the great Scharnhorst, spoke of the crucial role of decisiveness in warfare. It is a good principle, but not being susceptible to Romanticist influences, I understand it better than the post-Vienna Congress Clausewitz did. If you have a good cause, and can soundly outwit your adversary within the framework of the situation given to you, he is yours. You will defeat him, because your actions will occur in dimensions of physical geometry which he refuses to conceive as actually existing.

The Principle of the Economic Flank

On the world's stage today, we have two, contrasting views of "doing the unthinkable." In the one case, we have the conduct of President George Bush, who apparently has mastered the paradoxical feat of choosing the unthinkable unerringly, and repeatedly, without actually thinking. Then, we have my approach, which is to introduce principles of reason which others have refused to think about, until they were slapped in the face with the biggest, presently accelerating financial collapse in world history.

Obviously, the only useful thing to say under such circumstances, is to insist: "There is another way to see this challenge, outside the set of rules you have been misguided into trusting." In short: flank the problem! Do not be such a craven and opportunistic lick-spittle, that you refuse to raise the issue of the falseness of those axiomatic beliefs which your conversation-partner has been duped into trusting until now.

Say clearly, calmly, but emphatically and repeatedly: "There is a different way of thinking about economics; let me show you the error which has misled you into the present paradoxical situation."

The method which must be employed, is exactly that appropriate for discovering and proving the universal principle which solves an otherwise unconquerable paradox in physical science. You, yourself, must, first, undergo that experience of discovery and empirical validation of the needed principle. Then, you must use your own such experience, to provoke and induce the same cognitive process of discovering and validating the needed principle within the mind of another person.

You must act to teach him the Socratic truth-seeking way of Classical humanist methods of education, a way which is lost from virtually all existing classrooms in the Americas and Europe today. (Which is why, not only in former Governor George Bush's Texas, each generation of students is more ignorant than the previous one, in virtually all U.S.A. and European classrooms today.)

"You think you know something about economics? Let me show you where most of you made your big mistake."

Think back to Germany in the Fall of 1923, to those legendary days when a wheelbarrow full of 100 billions-marks banknotes could not meet the current price of a loaf of bread! Look at the energy-supplies, and their skyrocketting prices, in the state of California today. When the German government launched the hyperinflation of Summer and Fall of 1923, that government had an excuse for its lunatic monetary policy: they had French-occupation bayonets shoved down their throats. Who is shoving bayonets down the throat of Federal Reserve Chairman Greenspan and those others, who are shrieking demands for stoking up the monetary fires of U.S. hyperinflation today?

With that image in your mind, look at your neighbor, the idiot, who is screaming about "My money! My money! My money!" Look at that idiot in the U.S. Congress, who is glassy-eyed as his voice utters: "The market! It's the market! How is the market doing at this minute?" What about the quasi-homeless in Califor-

Bundesarchiv

Hyperinflation in Weimar Germany during the early 1920s: left, a banker counts the uncountable; right, a housewife lights her stove with worthless currency.

nia's Silicon Valley, who, until recent months and weeks, were living on "new economy" professionals' incomes, but could not afford to secure a rental or mortgage on even a high-priced tar-paper shack with a Hollywood exterior pasted on.

Like the fellow pushing a wheelbarrow full of paper money, in Autumn 1923 Germany, the simple question, "What can you buy, even if you have all that money?" takes all the magic out of the word "money." Meanwhile, since the high-point of recent market-indexes, the U.S. market has lost an obvious $5 trillions of "only money" values of "shareholdings," and, counting losses which have yet to be shown on the books, nearer to $10 trillions, or more. That in an economy whose official annual GDP is estimated in the order of $11 trillions a year. Except for those who should be swapping their suit-jackets for psychiatric-clinic camisoles, the magic of "The market!" is in the process of evaporating, as gloom takes over, to roam the halls of the Congress where Newton "Robespierre" Gingrich's psychotomimetic ("psychedelic") elation once reigned.

As the psychedelic orgy of "Our Money!" and "The Market!" collapses onto the sidewalk, next to the lawn of the home he once owned, the thoughts of the sobered mind turn to man's physical relationship to nature, the place where real values lie still, when even a currency like the U.S. dollar might be on the verge of going out of existence. How much will CNN and NBC have left to talk about, when a calm, like a neglected graveyard of lost dreams, settles on those once-so-boisterous stock exchanges? What happens to the current majority of the U.S. Supreme Court, on the day on which Antonin Scalia's Bogomil-like god, called "shareholder value," dies?

The principal lunacy, which has reigned over the U.S.A., its political institutions, and its economy, during the recent thirty-five-odd years, is the assumption that the production of physical wealth flows from the investment of money. That lunacy is about to be brought low, very low. Instead, we are forced to return to the wisdom of the reality, that it is the productive powers of labor which creates that increase of physical wealth, and related services, for which money is bought and sold.

That long-overdue fundamental shift, back to sanity, in axioms, is the key to the present world situation.

The principle is: If we can make the physical economy grow, and if we keep prices in line with long-term trends in per-capita output, then, with the resources of a sovereign nation-state, we can grow successfully out of any depth of financial collapse. If we reorganize the economy, using a sovereign government's unlimited authority to conduct bankruptcy reorganizations in keeping with our constitutional principle of the general welfare, then, under such use of the "Chapter 11" precedent, we can successfully make our way out of any financial crisis, including the worst financial collapse in world history, occurring right now, today.

Such is the principle of the flank. Excise the false belief which misled the nation into its present folly, and insert the valid principle from which our nation should never have departed, the principle which made Franklin Roosevelt the only truly successful U.S. President since William McKinley was assassinated.

To bring about that change in prevailing beliefs, the American people, at least a great number among them, must grasp the changes in principle, and see how those principles will work successfully to deal with the crisis at hand. We must spell that out for them. That will take much work on the part of many among us, but, we can, at least, begin now.

Let It Be a Successful Bankruptcy

The fundamental law of the United States' Federal Constitution, reposes in the Preamble, in which the so-called General Welfare clause is, as President Franklin Roosevelt emphasized in opposition to what he called "the American Tories" of his time, preeminent in respect to all economic and related practice.

To this end, we require the conversion of a sufficient portion of heretofore reluctant members of the U.S. Supreme Court, to put the Constitution above the Confederacy's Lockean principle of "shareholder value," to join with the majority of the Congress, and both with the sane members of the Executive branch, to order and support a process of "Chapter 11" mode of bankruptcy reorganization of the political-economy of our nation, and to enter into cooperation according to the same general principle and goals with cooperating other nations.

Without that mobilization of the political will of the U.S., neither this U.S. economy, nor, perhaps, even our republic, can be saved from an early extinction.

There is no middle ground; it is that clear cut, and the relevant decision correspondingly simple. That must be made painfully clear to every adolescent and adult person, whether they wish to face that reality, or not. Their future depends upon it.

The leading measures to be taken fall under six principal sub-headings, as follows.

A. Reorganization of Existing Accounts

Under no circumstances could all of the existing outstanding debts of the U.S.A. and world financial-monetary system ever be paid. Any attempt to enforce the continued imposition of that debt must necessarily loot the shrinking, remaining infrastructure and productive capacities of the world to the degree, that a general new dark age descends soon upon this planet as a whole. That is the first, hard decision which must be faced.

The greatest portion of that debt, must be written off. However, we must proceed to that result with careful attention to preserving the functioning of essential banking and other institutions, even if they were techni-cally hopelessly bankrupt. Above all, we must defend the integrity of the U.S. official debt, as Treasury Secretary Alexander Hamilton explained this point; all other debt is negotiable, subject to priorities dictated by the principle of the general welfare, giving priority to essential pensions, health care, and the modest savings of households and essential smaller business and related enterprises.

The action placing relevant entities under protection of a generalized "Chapter 11" bankruptcy reorganization shall be sudden, but, the resolution of the greatest portion of the generally frozen creditors' claims shall be deferred for final resolution to a suitable future time.

B. Forecasting Standards

In general, for reasons I have given elsewhere, the structuring of the process of reorganization in bankruptcy shall be designed for resolution of most of the outstanding claims over a period of about a quarter-century, or, a period of one basic economic cycle of the physical economy. Since it required thirty-five years to bring the once-prosperous economy to its present state of ruin, those who did so much to ruin it, should not consider their victims unreasonable in demanding that they should be allowed a quarter-century to re-build it.

During that interval, gradually released and frozen financial accounts held under bankruptcy protection, may be drawn up according to relevant law and procedure to give ordinary citizens, households, and enterprises, the means to conduct their own affairs without excessive red tape.

Also, to the degree this is prudent, the presumption that some portion of assets held in bankruptcy may prove redeemable, it may be arranged that some of that portion, at least, be treated as a non-performing but otherwise durable asset of certain banks and other financial institutions which are deemed essential to the general welfare, and to aid productive enterprises in orderly conduct of their business.

C. Credit-Expansion and Infrastructure

Under the conditions of bankruptcy reorganization produced by the present world financial collapse, the economic policy of the nation, must be focussed upon the use of regulated issues of public credit for increasing the ration of the total available labor-force employed in either the physical production of agricultural or industrial goods, development and maintenance of basic economic infrastructure, and essential services of material importance to both those functions and the welfare of the population.

This will not involve dumping monetary aggregate into financial markets, as is being done to hyperinflationary effect by Alan Greenspan, et al. Notably, since the chartered private corporation called the Federal Reserve System is itself bankrupt-in-fact, it must be taken under the protection in receivership of the U.S. Treasury, and its facilities utilized to provide the functions of a national bank, as the first and second national bank of the U.S.A. are a constitutional precedent for this. Although the implicit power of the U.S. Congress to authorize the issue of U.S. currency-notes, is involved in the creation of credit, public credit will flow into the market chiefly as credit to accounts within the banking system, under regulated and controlled conditions, as was done for U.S. defense production during the World War II mobilization.

Initially, the principal source of net growth of employment and physical net output will occur as public credit to development and maintenance of basic economic infrastructure by Federal or state programs, or through regulated public utilities. As much as 60% or more of the initial growth of our presently collapsed national physical economy will occur through those channels.

This will be accompanied by a large shift within the labor-force as a whole, away from financial and related kinds of services, and from relatively unskilled personal services employment, into higher qualities of employment in work related to the process of production of physical goods and essential infrastructure. This credit-catalyzed shift in the structural composition of the employment of the labor-force as a whole, will be among the leading levers in increasing the real average productivity, and net physical standard of living of the labor-force as a whole.

Large, well regulated credit-flows into development and maintenance of basic economic infrastructure, will spill over, increasingly, through contracts, as a stimulant for rebuilding the private productive sector.

D. Credit, Not Currency As Such

Under such conditions, there must be an immediate and drastic shift from the mentality of policies such as the inherently inflationary Kemp-Roth doctrine, to something akin to a "Kennedy investment tax-credit" policy.

The process of systemic ruin of the once-prosperous U.S. economy of the early 1960s, especially since the catastrophic 1977-1981 Carter Administration's orgy of deregulation, into the wreckage endured by the relatively impoverished lower eighty percentile of family-income brackets today, demonstrates again, had that lesson been needed, that pouring money into the pockets of both the wealthy and relatively less-unwealthy citizens, is not the way in which to promote actual net growth of the national tax-revenue base.

The way to go, is to maintain high rates of taxation on short- to medium-term financial capital gains, but to give advantageous tax treatment to medium- to long-term investments in the expansion and improvement of technologically progressive production of goods and in services relative to the welfare of the population and the promotion of technological progress in design and production of goods.

Similarly, we must have a relatively higher rate of interest charges on the borrowing of money, except for the protected categories of low-interest credit, and preferential tax treatments for investments and production in the relatively higher national economic and related interest. This serves, in addition to other purposes, to channel investment into medium- to long-term physical gains in productivity, and away from speculation, especially highly-leveraged speculation in the deadly area of short-term financial trading.

The emphasis must be on the theme of "prosperous austerity." Get by decently in the short term, grow, and prosper in the medium to long term. The notion that today's working family, shall have the benefit of increased productivity of the economy as their retirement age, and post-fifty health-care requirements increases, approaches, typifies a sound policy. Build a sound foundation, securely accumulated in growth of productivity, and secure financial assets, for a better future.

The image of wheelbarrows of money insufficient to buy a loaf of bread, should warn us that solid banked assets, especially long-term ones, if they are solid, is the place, not money or credit-card accounts, where a sensible nation builds up the bulk of its financial holdings.

E. The Technology Driver

Sane economists measure productivity in terms of the increase of society's power, per capita and per square-kilometer, in and over the universe we inhabit. This includes the improvement of the demographic characteristics of the typical family household.

This relationship of mankind to nature, is unique to the human species; no other species is capable of willfully increasing its potential relative (sustainable) population-density, as expressed in both per-capita and per-square-kilometer ratios. This is the characteristic of the human species which biogeochemist V.I. Vernadsky underlined, in his defining this inhabited planet of ours as a noösphere.

The primary source of this increased power of the human individual, is the discovery and application of valid new universal physical principles, the discoveries on which the development of improved technologies depends absolutely. Therefore, the only mode of actually sustainable economic growth of a society, is what is called a "science-driver" mode. This means, not only corresponding policies of education of the population as a whole, but also emphasis on increasing the rations of the total labor-force employed in fundamental scientific discovery, and in the translation of scientific progress into design, and improved methods of production, of products.

Government credit and taxation policies, must be attuned to emphasis upon that connection to sustainable real growth.

F. International Cooperation

This means that the U.S. must cooperate with some leading groups of nations abroad, to effect the same general type of reform of relevant international treaty-organizations, as that required for the internal financial crisis of the U.S.A.

We require, urgently, right now, a return to the kind of system of fixed parities and regulation which were employed in the two immediate post-war decades. Since the U.S.A. and a number of other nations, would be sufficient to impose such sudden reforms within an IMF system which is, by its present nature, an implicitly bankrupt institution, such a reform is a feasible one, especially if the U.S.A. were to participate in bringing it about.

As I have emphasized repeatedly in other published locations, the key to a durable U.S. economic recovery, is a durable international economic recovery. The key to the world economy as a whole, lies in the urgency of U.S. cooperation with key nations of Eurasia, for a general Eurasian development, whose benefits would be directed into spill-overs into areas such as Africa and Central and South America. This must emphasize the increased output of high-technology exports, especially of a machine-tool quality, to those parts of the world which are relatively deficient in their own present capacity to meet such urgent internal consumption requirements.

This cooperation has several leading impacts for the U.S. economy itself.

First, it raises the priority for expansion of the science-driver potentials of the U.S.A., Europe, and Japan, most notably. In other words, the need for such technology in the world at large, must raise the level of priority for the quantity and rate of such scientific and related investment and employment in the U.S. itself.

In general, international cooperation along such lines, means a base-line for relevant policy-shaping and economic agreements of not less than a generation, approximately a quarter-century.

Say, 2026, by which time we should have put the worst of the present situation behind us, at least if we can now discover the good sense to adopt such a change in our policy.